BRANDING IN ASIA

*The Creation, Development, and
Management of Asian Brands
for the Global Market*

BRANDING IN ASIA

The Creation, Development, and Management of Asian Brands for the Global Market

Paul Temporal

John Wiley & Sons (Asia) Pte Ltd

Singapore   New York   Chichester
Brisbane   Toronto   Weinheim

Copyright © 2000 John Wiley & Sons (Asia) Pte Ltd
2 Clementi Loop, #02-01, Singapore 129809

This publication is designed to provide accurate and authoritative information in
regard to the subject matter covered. It is sold with the understanding that the Publisher
is not engaged in rendering professional services. If professional advice or other expert
assistance is required, the services of a competent professional person should be sought.

Other Wiley Editorial Offices

John Wiley & Sons, Inc., 605 Third Avenue, New York, NY 10158-0012, USA
John Wiley & Sons Ltd, Baffins Lane, Chichester, West Sussex PO19 1UD, England
John Wiley & Sons (Canada) Ltd, 22 Worcester Road, Rexdale, Ontario M9W 1L1, Canada
John Wiley & Sons Australia Ltd, 33 Park Road (PO Box 1226), Milton, Queensland 4046,
Australia
Wiley-VCH, Pappelallee 3, 69469 Weinheim, Germany

Library of Congress Cataloging-in-Publication Data:

Temporal, Paul.
    Branding in Asia: the creation, development, and management of Asian brands for the
global market / Paul Temporal.
        p. cm.
    Includes bibliographical references and index.
    ISBN 0-471-83576-5 (cloth : alk. paper)
        1. Brand name products—Case studies. 2. Marketing—Case studies. 3. Competition,
International—Case studies.   I. Title.

HD69.B7.T45   1999
658.8'27'095 21; aa05 09-24-dc99   99-049104

Typeset in 11/15 point, Goudy by Linographic Services Pte Ltd
Printed in Singapore by Siak Wah Press Pte Ltd
10 9 8 7 6 5 4 3 2 1

Dedication
To Evelyn and Maria
with love

Contents

Acknowledgments

There are so many people who have helped me in different ways to write this book, but special thanks are due to the following:

Alan Goh	Lee Kwok Cheong
Bettina Chua Abdullah	Lim Chuan Poh
C.Y. Cheong	Mark Singleton
Chris Harris	Peter Hamilton
Daniel Binns	Professor John A. Quelch
Datuk Paddy Bowie	Roland Chew
Datuk Yong Poh Kon	Sabrina Chin Su Fern
Geoff Stecyk	Shelley Siu
Guy Murphy	Sim Hai Yeun
Ho Kwon Ping	Stan Shih
John Madsen	Theresa Chew-Tan
Judy Wong Lee Yoon	Yong Pang Chaun

and many others who have helped me in one way or another.

I would also like to thank the following organizations for their case studies, information and co-operation.

Acer	Malaysian Mosaics
Asia Business Forum	McCann-Erickson
Banyan Tree Hotels and Resorts	National Computer Systems
BBH Asia Pacific	North West Arts Board
BMW	Orient Pacific Century
Boon Rawd Brewery	*Rugby World*
British Airways	Starbucks
British High Commission	Singapore Airlines
British-Malaysian Industry and	Singapore Telecom
Trade Association	Sitra Wood
CNBC	Southern Unit Trust
Expressions International	The British Council
Haw Par Healthcare Ltd	The British Tourist Authority

My thanks also go to Nick Wallwork for giving me the opportunity to write this book, Janis Soo and Elizabeth Daniel for helping me appear a better writer than I actually am, and the Wiley Asia team for their support and encouragement.

Preface

This book is about building brands. Its focus is Asia because there is now great interest from Asian companies in branding. This newfound curiosity has arisen partly because companies have seen how the world's most powerful brands have withstood the onslaught of recession, and partly because they are now beginning to think more strategically, taking a longer-term view of business growth rather than concentrating solely on next year's results.

There are few powerful brands with Asian origins, apart from the giant Japanese companies that have been concentrating successfully on brand building for the last two or three decades. Japanese companies are not featured strongly in the Asian case material. Instead, I have chosen to feature several Asian brands from other countries that are in the midst of their brand-building efforts; some are at an early stage of brand development while others have achieved some notable success already. But, these are not really large companies. I have chosen to write the book in this manner to show that size is not an impediment to building a brand—good brands can be created by small companies as well as large ones. I have, however, included cases of well-known international brands from which I feel lessons can be learned by Asian companies. Also, throughout the text, many local and international brands are used as illustration, where needed.

I would like to share this message with companies in Asia, where I have worked for the last 14 years: Asia still has the potential to dominate world trade during the next few decades. But, it will be companies that are starting to develop or are developing powerful brands now, which will find themselves as leaders in the global market of the future. I hope this book will provide managers with practical ideas that will help them gain a strategic competitive advantage, and create brand names that will make their companies the envy of the world, just as the western brands are now.

Foreword

Developing an Asian brand is not easy. The poor image of "Made in Asia", coupled with small domestic markets have been the source of problematic business growth for many Asian companies.

In positioning Asian brands we must be innovative to overcome our inherent disadvantages. Although the branding world is very crowded now, dynamic markets usually bring a lot of new opportunities of which Asian businesses can take advantage. However, only innovative technology, products, and services that can provide high quality and value to customers will sustain businesses in the new competitive era.

Limited market space for Asian companies is another challenge. Domestic markets in Asia are mainly dominated by Western brands. However, I truly believe that while technology is global, markets are local. Asian companies can start to build their brands in their domestic and regional markets, where they understand the consumers. After successfully developing the quantity and quality of business, and with sufficient resources, companies can then begin to penetrate the more remote markets. This is a good way to start building a global brand.

Companies wishing to build strong brands must be persistent. Only consistent, innovative capability and communications, with the right positioning, can impress people and build brand loyalty. Building a strong corporate brand requires significant investment, sometimes at the expense of short-term profitability. As Paul Temporal points out, the returns on brand investment are well worth the extra effort.

Brand-building in Asia for the global market in the 21st century is important because brand sells. This book provides a very valuable introduction to all the necessary brand-building concepts, in plain language, to help executives in their awareness of how to develop and manage their brands. Most importantly, the case studies give examples of good branding practice, and add fun to the study of brand development.

Stan Shih
Chairman & CEO
The Acer Group

Introduction

THE NEED FOR STRONG ASIAN BRANDS

"Buildings age and become dilapidated.
Machines wear out.
People die.
But what live on are the brands."

So said Sir Hector Laing, who as group chief executive officer of United Biscuits plc ran the United Kingdom-based company with a huge portfolio of brands. It is a wonderful quotation because it is so true. And, if there is one overriding message in this book, then this quotation is it.

This message is relevant for turbulent times as well. Periods of profound and rapid change, like what we are experiencing now as the 20th century draws to a close, put a premium on the ability to survive. Unfortunately, many companies go under. A surprising number of corporations that were on the Fortune 500 list a decade ago are no longer on it, while the current economic crisis has eliminated others entirely.

But, Coca-Cola is still on the prestigious list. At over 100 years old, it is probably the world's most successful brand, and is likely to be around for the whole of the next century. The top brands of the 1920s—Colgate, Kellogg's, Kodak, and others—have maintained their lead to this day in many disparate and changing markets. They are still leading brands, despite the many worldwide changes that have affected every business and being managed by various people over the years. Strong brands are amazingly durable, enduring many challenges. They are the *real McCoys*.

Brand longevity is becoming increasingly relevant—more than it has ever been—as the world approaches the new millennium, an era of unprecedented change, upheaval, and uncertainty. This change is strategic, unlike the incremental change of more predictable times, and therefore, requires a strategic response. Brand building is exactly such a response. If successful, it can be the strongest weapon in a company's armory and the best guarantee of corporate survival. The challenge that lies ahead is that of change management.

A catalog of worldwide changes

Recalling the past 30 years, we note how much the world has changed. In the late 1960s, man landed on the moon; in the 1990s, he landed technology on Mars. In the 1960s, Communism was a world force to be reckoned with; in the 1990s, it has nearly disappeared. From the mass entry of the personal computer in the early 1980s to the power of the Internet today, everything is changing rapidly. In the world of business, some markets are declining, while new ones are being born and growing quickly. It was only in the latter half of the 20th century that DNA was recognized as life's building block, giving birth to a new industry— genetic engineering. Progress in the industry has since flourished so rapidly, with many new products promising new prevention and cures for critical illnesses, and cloning is now a distinct possibility, having been achieved with animals. Technology drives this fast-changing world, and many observers say we are surely entering a post-industrial era that will transform society more radically, profoundly, and disturbingly than the Industrial Revolution.

Today's businesses are subjected to a great deal of turbulence and accelerating changes. Unfortunately, change has not benefited everyone. Asian companies feel the impact of this change to a greater degree than others elsewhere in the world, as they try to catch up and overtake the competition. Since 1997, they have also felt the tremendous pressures of the economic roller coaster. Catastrophic currency and foreign debt problems have all but broken many Asian economies and made life a struggle for the majority of Asian businesses. But, failure cannot be blamed entirely on external circumstances; companies must accept some responsibility.

To a certain extent, poor management is to blame. Many Asian companies have been diagnosed to be suffering from strategic myopia, as some settle for complacency and short-term gains. Others have joined the desperate pursuit of operational efficiency through quality programs, re-engineering, customer service, and other prevailing management trends that inadvertently failed to deliver high-level performance. An independent study published in 1998 of the impact of the implementation of ISO 9000 procedures in manufacturing companies in an Asian country showed that successful implementation of this type of total quality management program does not necessarily produce any significant increase in profitability; in some cases, profitability actually declined.

Disillusioned by these once desirable activities, Asian companies are now adopting a more strategic focus, centered on long-term survival and profitability. Although faced with a dearth of solutions, they still tend to neglect the one answer that can provide the security and profitability they seek—the creation of powerful international brands. Branding helps companies position themselves strategically for the future and compete effectively with the global giants that dominate world markets. Had Asian companies established international brands, many of their problems arising from the economic crisis may not have been so severe. However, developing successful brands is not an easy task. There is no quick fix, and most companies do not have the relevant experience or knowledge necessary to embark on this route. There is a whole new technology involved, which this book endeavors to expound.

In the 1990s, the media paid an increasing amount of attention to brand power, and this raised the awareness level of many companies of what brands can accomplish. As a result, a growing number of Asian companies are committed to developing strong brands. They are also realizing the importance of good image management, having suffered from the adverse economic situation and the residual baggage of damaged national images caused by recession. So all in all, Asian companies are beginning to realize what branding really means, the benefits it can bring—especially in terms of increased corporate worth—and the consequences of not pursuing it.

As a prelude to the main theme—and to put in perspective the market dynamics that have affected companies in recent times and catalog the changes that have implications for branding in Asia—seven major world market trends are explained.

SEVEN WORLD MARKET TRENDS

The significant elements of change encountered over the last two decades can be categorized into seven world market trends that affect today's businesses. These are:

- the breakdown of market boundaries
- globalization and the development of global brands
- increasing market fragmentation
- product diversity and shorter life cycles
- greater customer sophistication
- digital business
- economic instability and market volatility

The breakdown of market boundaries

Traditionally, markets have been self-contained. But, the advent of new technology has allowed many companies to move into markets that were previously unknown and inaccessible. Industry crossovers, as they are sometimes called, are not unusual anymore.

Another contributory factor to the breakdown of market boundaries is deregulation. It is difficult to find any industry that has escaped deregulation in recent years; international legislation such as the initiatives of the World Trade Organization and Asean Free Trade Area have hurried this process along. Over the next 10 to 15 years, further legislation will insure that trade protection is an anachronism, and this will add to the considerable pressures already felt by Asian businesses, forcing them to fight more competitively with the international giants.

A third cause for the erosion of market boundaries is the increase in the number of strategic alliances. Despite the risks of incompatibility in these forced marriages, strategic alliances continue to prove attractive to companies by offering them global reach and access to new and distant markets. The Star Alliance and the One network in the airline industry are examples of alliances offering these benefits.

Globalization and the development of global brands

Globalization is both a current boardroom buzzword and a commercial reality, as more companies seek to achieve a worldwide presence. An influential factor has been the standardization of buying patterns, with people in most countries inclined towards similar products and services. Travel to any major city and you will see familiar fashion goods, fast-food outlets, motor vehicles, hi-fi systems, financial services, etc. This makes it easier for companies to produce and market generic products that deliver volume sales at a lower cost base. There is no doubt that this phenomenon has been a catalyst in the development of global brand strategies.

Globalization has also been propelled by the frequent mega-mergers of recent times, including that between Citicorp and The Travelers Group, and between Daimler-Benz and Chrysler. Other companies have not acquired businesses in such huge chunks, but have systematically picked up stakes in companies around the world in their drive for global status, for example, British Telecom in Malaysia with Binariang, and in Singapore with Star Hub.

Another inducement to globalization has been the opening up of previously restricted markets, such as those in Eastern Europe. Again, this has favored established brand leaders and encouraged some of the fast-growing companies to broaden their international market coverage. Globalization poses significant challenges to Asian companies—not many of which can claim to be global players—in two ways. First, Asian companies have to cope with increasing competition in their domestic markets from international brands. Second, due to limited domestic consumption, Asian companies have to try to break into world markets, which tend to be dominated by two or three leading companies.

Increasing market fragmentation

Having said earlier that there is a trend towards increasing standardization of buying patterns, it seems contradictory to now say that markets are becoming more fragmented. However, within broad markets, there is as increasing number of customer groups that identify themselves by their distinctive needs and wants. So, it is true to say that although customers generally tend to buy similar generic products and services, they are demanding that these be tailored to their specific requirements. Companies have reacted to this by shifting their stance from mass marketing to mass customization.

Product diversity and shorter life cycles

One of the reactions to greater competition is product development, made easier by the speed of technological advances. This, coupled with the demand for more customized products, has resulted in product proliferation, so much so that customers are sometimes bewildered by the wide range of choices they are offered. A consequent problem is the increasing difficulty to produce a product or service that is enduringly different. To use marketing jargon, unique selling propositions (USPs) are hard to find and sustain. While technological advances spur further innovation and become more freely available to everyone, leadership in product innovation is more difficult to achieve, but easier to emulate, and therefore, short-lived.

The rate of technological change is staggering. In some markets, product life cycles have been shortened to a matter of months instead of years, as is the case with personal computers (PCs); PCs currently have a life cycle of only six months, after which they become obsolete. As a result, companies are caught in a trap. On the one hand, they cannot afford to be lagging in the race for product development or enhancement, and on the other, to keep ahead in the race, they have to invest heavily in technology with its built-in obsolescence, and thus, aim to gain mandatory rapid returns at the same time.

Greater customer sophistication

Nowadays, people are generally more well educated, possess greater spending power, and have better lifestyles than before. They are also more demanding in their determination to secure value for money. This newfound independence has manifested itself in a greater tendency by customers to exercise their right to choose, resulting in consumer loyalty becoming more fragile, and shifting from ordinary companies and products to powerful brands.

Digital business

As the world moves rapidly into the digital age, companies have to adapt to new ways of doing business, such as marketing on the Internet and other electronic media. Sophisticated infocommunications technologies drive these new marketing channels, and while some companies are happily adjusting to it, others are choosing to ignore it. With these new marketing channels, the problem faced by companies is in recreating the relationship and association with the consumer that were enjoyed previously through the old marketing channels. The new channels do not facilitate the meeting of customers with company personnel face to face, but instead allow customers to view the products on a computer screen.

Economic instability and market volatility

No economy has been spared from the destabilizing forces of recent times, with Asian economies suffering more than most. As economic growth is cyclical—rendering markets unpredictable—it is highly unlikely that companies will ever again experience long periods of stability that they have known in the past. However, companies that appear to had been least affected by the chaos are those with powerful brand names.

These seven trends are continuing to roll forward, hence, accelerating the rate of change and creating more turbulence in world markets. What can be predicted about the future is that

- change will continue to accelerate
- uncertainty will get stronger
- markets will become more fragmented and dynamic
- customers will get more sophisticated and demanding
- competition will get tougher
- survival will become more difficult

Companies will also have to deal with issues that they did not have to confront before.

EIGHT STRATEGIC ISSUES FOR THE 21ST CENTURY

Eight urgent and strategic questions face many Asian companies: How can they

- gain global recognition?
- reduce their dependence on contract manufacturing and other less desirable alliances?
- access and penetrate new markets?
- avoid their products being seen and bought as commodities?
- reduce their costs and increase their value?
- establish a presence in new and emerging industries?
- secure long-term profits and growth, and survive the hard times?
- break parity and stand out from the crowd?

The answer to these questions is: the creation, development, and management of international brands. The reasons for this can be seen by examining the power and rewards that brands can bring to companies.

The market power of brands

The market power of brands can be astonishing. Here are some ways in which strong brands can transform ordinary businesses into elite ones.

Survival in adverse conditions

This attribute of strong branding is a critical issue for Asian companies, especially after discovering that the strengths they thought they had were vulnerable during the recent economic meltdown. Strong branding represents one of the best defenses against adverse economic and other market conditions. During the recessionary period of the 1990s, none of the powerful brands represented in Asia fell. Looking back at previous hard times around the world, we observe the same picture. For instance, in the early 1980s when gasoline prices rose dramatically as a result of the oil crisis, thus bringing about the failure of many car-manufacturing establishments, only Mercedes-Benz had increased its sales.

Longevity

Strong brands are endurable, and longevity is a much sought-after attribute in Asia—pursued and valued in all aspects of life, not least of all in business. When nurtured and well looked after, brands can insure corporate immortality. In Asia, there is a healthy respect for and wisdom associated with older age.

In Vietnam, despite a 20-year war when all advertisements connected to the U.S. were banned, there is still tremendous recall of powerful brands. These days, despite low disposable-income levels, the typical Vietnamese family treat on Sunday is an American fast-food meal down at their favorite street. As can be seen, American brands have overcome the prejudice of recent and former enemies: strong brands survive against the odds.

Transportability across national cultures

A powerful brand can cut across national boundaries and cultures with great ease. Coca-Cola has a presence in virtually every country in the world. In Asia, where food with its subtle spices and sauces is a gourmet's delight, families still flock to McDonald's. This is not to say that foreign brands do not have to adapt their products and marketing activities to suit local conditions, cultures, and tastes—they do. But, these successful foreign brands seem to generate excitement and emotional response from every audience introduced to it. Nearly every capital city in the world has its prestigious street lined with shops and boutiques carrying the big international brand names. In general, brands are synonymous with sophistication and glamour, and in traditional societies, brands represent progress and are symbols of the modern world.

Greater distribution power

Companies carrying powerful international brands have gained access to many global markets, and in the course of doing this, have managed to secure strong distribution channels. This makes it easier for them to gain effective distribution for the other brands they have in their portfolios, i.e. brands that do not share the same status as the powerful brand.

Crossing market boundaries

The strength of powerful brand names allows them to venture into different industries. Dunhill, for example, has moved from cigarettes to high-class fashion products, and Virgin has an airline and is in financial services, rail travel, and many other industries.

Accessing and penetrating new markets is also easier when riding on a powerful brand name, as Marks & Spencer (M&S) found out when it made its initial entry into the financial sector through the launch of its unit trust in the late 1980s. The M&S brand name—synonymous with quality and value for money—carried this new business to instant success, even though the company had no previous track record in the financial services. So successful was this move into unit trusts, that it outsold the entire unit-trust industry's earnings for the year within the first three months of operations.

Staff motivation, recruitment, and loyalty

The sheer reputation and image of the big international brands are high motivators for employees, who like to be associated with world-famous names. This encourages good morale and employee loyalty, while attracting quality staff. Many managerial executives aim to work for the top brands because of the experience they expect to gain: the best managers want to work for the best companies.

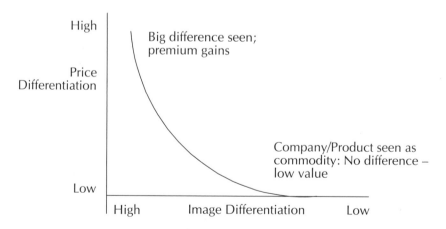

Figure 1: Branding adds differentiation through intangible values such as personality.

Moving away from commodity status

A major 21st century strategic issue for businesses in Asia will be how to break out of parity. An increasing number of products and services are virtually indistinguishable from each other, and the only way to break out of the mold (commodity status) is by incorporating value into consumers' perceptions of the product or service. This is what branding is about. It is often the intangible values built into an ordinary product or service that help to stand out from the crowd and command premium price.

The financial rewards of brands

Powerful brands provide long-term security and growth, higher sustainable profits, and increased asset value because they achieve:

- competitive differentiation
- premium prices
- higher sales volumes
- economies of scale and reduced costs
- greater security of demand

For these reasons, the creation of powerful international brands is the road to travel by Asian businesses. This is the strategic path that has been missing from many boardroom discussions over recent years, and one which could possibly have saved a number of companies. The attention now being paid to the valuation of brands shows just how substantial contribution to the profitability and worth of companies can be. For instance, it is worthwhile to note that the US$8.67 billion merger between British American Tobacco plc (BAT) and Rothmans International BV still will not bring the newly merged BAT entity close to Philip Morris (owner of the megabrand, Marlboro) in terms of profitability or return on assets, even though BAT will have over 240 brands in its newly merged portfolio. BAT still will not have a true global brand, while powerful world brands like Marlboro reap huge rewards.

One can even invest in entertainer brands. David Bowie was the first rock star to issue a bond. Brand valuation has become a business in its own right.

THE VALUATION OF BRANDS

Marketers have for decades regarded brands as major company assets. The concentration of attention by chief executives and financial analysts on the worth of brands, however, is a relatively recent phenomenon, begun in the 1980s when a series of acquisitions were made. During those few years, some ground-breaking financial decisions were made. For example, Reckitt & Colman (R&C) acquired the Airwick Group from Ciba-Geigy at £165 million of which £55.8 million of assets were entered into its balance sheet to recognize the value of the Airwick brands. In 1998, Rank Hovis McDougall, under pressure from a hostile takeover bid, included R&C's brands as an intangible capital asset item in its balance sheet to the value of £678 million. In the same year, Nestlé paid £2.5 billion for Rowntree in spite of Rowntree's net asset value being only £300 million, and Philip Morris paid four times the net asset value of Kraft in its takeover.

This spate of acquisitions started off a debate, which is still underway, as to how, not why, brands should be valued. Since then, many other companies have also provided for brands in their accounts, including Cadbury Schweppes, United Biscuits, Ladbroke, and other prominent world players, because:

- stronger balance sheets are good for raising funds, loan collateral, and stock price
- gearing ratios are reduced by including the value of brands
- brand valuation helps stave off competitive attacks and hostile acquisition moves
- it makes companies more attractive, giving them the ability to negotiate a higher price should they want to sell
- it gives a truer picture of the total business and its current and potential worth

Assessing the value of a portfolio of brands means assessing the brands independently, as entities in their own right. This can be beneficial because:

- they can then be traded separately, and this is essential for licensing and franchising, for instance
- it makes for better brand comparisons, helping companies to decide how to allocate resources most effectively
- the nature of brand valuation provides marketers with valuable information on current and future brand profitability, market share, positional strength, loyalty, and other measures of success

Clearly, there is considerable benefit in assessing the financial worth of brands, and brand valuation is itself a growing business. But, there is still no agreed way of doing it. Valuation is not easy as a great deal of brand value is of a distinctly intangible nature, manifested in elements such as brand loyalty and emotional associations held by consumers. In the past, the term "goodwill" had accounted for some estimates of brand value, but attempts are now being made to assess brand equity more systematically and comprehensively.

No agreed methodology

Other books discuss this issue in detail, but the rationale for assessing the worth of brands is agreed by all. The basis of any calculation of brand worth is to establish the relative strength of the brand. Unless this is accomplished, it is impossible to determine with any degree of accuracy the reliability of a brand's future cash flow. It is the anticipated cash flow multiplied by the brand earnings or profit that gives the real picture of what the brand is worth currently and what future ownership of it will be worth.

The assessment of brand worth involves identifying future earnings projections (allowing for risk and inflation) and applying a multiple to past earnings as a discount rate to future cash flow. It is a rigorous procedure, which involves measuring the strength of brands on several performance factors that are often weighted. These factors may include:

- brand strength—the ability to influence the market in matters such as price and distribution, and resistance to attack
- market leadership—in terms of share over time, awareness levels, and esteem
- loyalty and retention—this has a bearing on long-term survival
- market situation—this is the growth of, volatility of, and barriers of entry to the market
- global potential—the brand's ability to be international, as opposed to merely national or regional
- innovation—the brand's ability to keep itself modern and relevant to its market or markets
- brand investment—the value and consistency of support for the brand in terms of marketing and communications
- protection—legal and trade protection of the brand

There are critics of every method (and there are several methods), who say that it is impossible to estimate with any degree of accuracy what a brand is worth. One of the problems is that not all factors may be relevant to each brand at any particular point in time. However, to ignore the value of brands is to vastly underestimate the true worth of companies. And, many believe that the currently available methods are a great improvement on past attempts that focused merely on "goodwill" guessing.

The message here for Asian companies is that focusing on short-term profits is clearly necessary, but it would be unwise not to concentrate on the long-term health of the company, which could bring vast rewards with the building of strong brands. There has to be a balance.

CAN ASIAN COMPANIES DEVELOP INTERNATIONAL BRANDS?

There are some who say that Asian companies would find it incredibly difficult to build international and global brands. Their reason is that most of the world markets and the product categories in those markets are already dominated by powerful global brands. They say that Asian companies lag so far behind these megabrands that they will never catch up. Furthermore, they claim that Asian companies have to overcome significant global consumer perceptions of sub-par quality and other concerns relating to country of origin of the brand. There is a lot of truth in these comments, and it will be no easy task for Asian companies to develop strong brands of their own, but it is the very nature of the fast-changing business world that can help them. There is no hard and fast rule anymore, and innovation no longer belongs to the privileged few.

There are many Asian corporate leaders with the vision necessary to harness technology and ideas, both of which are freely available. And, global niche-markets are available to those who can move in quickly, as speed is not a strength of many existing global giants. There is more than just hope despite the sub-par quality perceptions associated with Asian-made products. Japanese companies have managed to overcome the initial negative perceptions of sub-par quality. Similarly, other Asian companies can do the same, and indeed are doing. However, there are many other aspects of branding that Asian companies have to improve upon in order to achieve international recognition. In particular, corporate thinking has to stop focusing on short-term profits and concentrate on long-term brand building, which is a strategic discipline in its own right. So, there is confidence that Asian companies can develop international brands, and they would be ill-advised not to do so.

This book highlights the need for Asian companies to work hard on the branding issue. Brand development is a realistic opportunity, and this book shows in a practical way how Asian companies can go about it. It has been written as a tribute to the few Asian companies—the trailblazers—that are attempting to develop strong international brands, and as a guide for those that wish to do so. It expands on methodology, and makes use of role models. Good examples of strong branding from around the world abound. International brands are a dime a dozen, but successful Asian brands are rare, especially if Japan is excluded. This book highlights the lessons to be learned from both. In the book are several case studies featuring international and Asian brands, but the giant brands of Japan are not featured as Asian cases, as they have attained already international or global status. Such brands include Sony, Canon, Toyota, and Fujitsu. However, Japanese brands are referred to in the text from time to time to illustrate points of good branding practice.

Outside Japan, Acer is arguably one of Asia's most successful international brands. As the first case study in this book, it has been chosen as an example of how one entrepreneur created an international brand in a highly competitive market within a relatively short space of time. It epitomizes what Asian companies can achieve, and how they can stand out in a crowded market place. The brand is still developing, but has the firm foundations necessary for it to become a global brand.

The Tiger Balm case study is chosen as an example of how an ordinary but good quality product can — through careful branding and marketing — become an international brand. It highlights the skillful use of heritage and modernity, and the extension of the brand through positioning to access different target audiences.

Case Study 1

ACER
The story of a successful Asian brand

Stan Shih is a national hero in Taiwan; Acer is a successful international brand.

The computer industry is one of the most competitive in the world, having always been dominated by giants such as IBM. So, how has a Taiwanese company become the third largest manufacturer of PCs in the world, creating a respected, and sometimes feared, brand? How has the company managed to break away from the "Made in Taiwan" image, which like that of many countries in Asia has been associated with sub-standard products?

The answer is, of course, the careful construction of a strong brand image. From the very beginning, Shih realized that this was the great challenge, and he positioned his products more at the higher end of the market than any other Taiwanese products had been previously. For example, when entering the

Japanese market, he priced his products the same as theirs to avoid the poor-quality image associated with lower-priced products. This was an important signal emitted by the brand— that Acer-branded products were not to be classified as commodities.

Acer Computer has always spent huge sums of money on research and development, and in this respect, tends to follow the Japanese technology companies. Shih believes in "innovalue"—using innovation to create value in the design and production of cutting-edge products—and leading the industry. It is Shih's company that has actually positioned the PC as an aesthetically pleasing home appliance, and this philosophy is summed up in the new corporate mission statement: "Fresh Technology Enjoyed by Everyone, Everywhere." Fresh does not imply new but the best, namely, proven high-value, low-risk technology that is affordable to everyone, and has a long lifespan. Fresh also refers to innovation based on mature technology that is user-friendly, reasonably priced, and enjoyed by everyone, everywhere. Acer Computer has a long history of innovation, and continues to add to this strength at every opportunity.

Acer Computer's aim is to become more consumer-oriented, as it believes that PCs will become electronic consumer-products with a wider range of uses and applications in the areas of communications, entertainment, and education. Acer Computer, therefore, has to become an expert in consumer electronics as well as personal computing. Shih refers to this as a shift from being "technology-centric" to "consumer-centric." The computer industry has always been the former— emphasizing products more than people. Acer Computer is thus re-positioning itself to become a customer-centric intellectual-property and service company, as signified by its new slogan: "Acer, Bringing People and Technology Together." To Shih, intellectual property is the value added to the product. Acer Computer adds value by enhancing consumer perceptions of the benefit or value of a product, based on know-how, packaging, design, accessibility, comfort, user-friendliness, and niche solutions—the tangible qualities of its products. This is how Acer Computer is building on its already strong international brand, into a global brand. It wants to help people to enjoy their work and their lives.

One way in which Acer Computer is trying to manage the perceptions of its audience and getting them to think of the company as a major player is through more international exposure, such as its US$10-million sponsorship of the 1998 Asian Games. Acer's technology was recognized as giving a "perfect performance" by the 13th Asian Games Organizing Committee, and it succeeded in bringing the company greater international exposure. Another way Acer Computer is managing customers' perception of the company is by partnering overseas companies. By doing this, Acer Computer achieves its overall philosophy of "global brand, local touch," and also hopes to further the perception of being a global brand.

However, Acer still has to make the leap from being a regional brand to a global one. Although the company manufactures computers for IBM and other major companies, it does not get due credit. In 1998, it was ranked third in the world as a PC manufacturer, but occupied only eighth spot in brand sales. Since then, it has moved to seventh place, according to the company. In the largest single market in the world—the United States—Acer's market share in 1998 was less than 5%.

Acer Computer has to cross the bridge, from world-class manufacturer and regional-market leader to global player. If the result depends solely on Stan Shih's enthusiasm, energy, and ambition, then there will be no doubt about the outcome. But consumers, both corporate and individual, make global brands happen, and therein lies the challenge of changing and managing their perceptions.

Brand strengths: founder/CEO's vision, cost leadership, quality products, consumer focus, innovation.

Case Study 2

TIGER BALM
An ordinary Asian product becomes an international brand

Tiger Balm is an interesting example of a truly Asian brand that has gained international recognition. It is a herbal ointment remedy passed down through the generations, with its origin in the imperial courts of China, whose warlords and emperors needed relief from aches, pains, and a variety of other ailments.

The Aw family were the ones who developed the product and the brand. Patriarch Aw Chu Kin passed his knowledge of Chinese medicine to his sons, Boon Par (meaning gentle leopard) and Boon Haw (meaning gentle tiger). The "Tiger" in the brand name comes from Boon Haw's name. Boon Haw was also the pioneer marketer of the product. The company name of Haw Par comes from last names of both brothers. Tiger Balm is now an international brand based in Singapore, with sales in excess of S$100 million. Control of Haw Par and Tiger Balm has passed, as it inevitably does in such situations, from the family to a large corporate group. However, the packaging still retains the old reproduction photographs of the two brothers, with their names in Chinese and English.

The springing tiger logo, created by Boon Haw, has always been the trademark of the brand, successfully creating a high degree of awareness and recall in global markets. The packaging—consisting of an official-looking, imitation paper-seal as the cover over the small hexagonal jars and round cans—has made the product so unique that it stands out easily from other international competitors, of which there are many. Yet, the brand has managed to look modern while retaining its heritage.

As discussed in an earlier section, to build a brand, a company must also have a quality product, and Tiger Balm scores well in this aspect. The original recipe for the ointment has been enhanced with additives from Western and Chinese medicines. It has multi-usage positioning and application—relieving headaches to muscular sprains and aches; both young and old people use it. It is also positioned as a sports-injury product, endorsed by sports personalities, thus giving it a wider customer base.

Tiger Balm has a tremendous heritage following in Asia, and it is now successfully marketed in over 70 countries worldwide. It has made the leap from its Asian beginnings as a folk remedy to a truly international brand.

Brand strengths: tiger symbolism, unique packaging, heritage, multiple usage created by strong target-user, multi-positioning strategy.

(Reproduced with permission from Haw Par Healthcare Ltd)

An advertisement for the range of Tiger Balm products

1

Understanding Brands

The origin of branding goes back a long way. Brands were originally distinguishing marks placed by one means or another by owners on their products and animals, if one recalls the old western movies. Brands still fulfill the basic function of differentiation today, but the techniques of branding have progressed enormously. Branding is now a sophisticated process that puts together and sustains a complex mixture of attributes and values, many of which are intangible. The objective of branding is to produce a unique and attractive offering that meets both the rational and the emotional needs of customers in a better way than the competition.

Some brands fail, while others succeed. It is difficult to analyze the determinants in each case; such is the complexity of the art of branding. Even companies that have developed famous brands will not be able to give a precise answer or show a grand plan road-mapping their success. In the end, it is the consumer that chooses. Perhaps our inability to pinpoint why one brand is amazingly successful while another remains mediocre, is a reflection of our inability to discover what drives human behavior and how people make their choices. It is this mystery that makes branding both intriguing and exciting. Market research and logical decision-making can lead marketers to certain conclusions, but there is no way that the success of a brand can be predicted. Even long after the launch of a newly branded product or service, this unpredictability remains over time. Hence, brand management becomes essential and demands constant vigilance.

However, certain agreed principles and techniques have proven to be fundamental to successful brand building, and they narrow the odds of losing the branding game. As we now have the benefit of knowing what customers have seen and believed about the world's most famous brands, and what the companies that have built them up have done, we are able to use a practical approach to increase our understanding of how brands work. But, we will first begin with definitions.

WHAT IS A BRAND?

Names, logos, and other visual identity

It is best to start by explaining what a brand is not, in order to dispel some common misconceptions. Based on the origin of branding (as discussed at the start of this chapter), it is not surprising to find that some people think that the basis of modern-day branding is mainly the use of names, logos, trademarks, and slogans. This is true only to the extent that they are all used to distinguish companies and individuals from each other in terms of what they offer. The consistent use of a brand name, symbol, or logo makes the brand instantly recognizable to consumers, and can bring to mind the personality of the brand, and its associations. However, although the visual element of design is an important aspect of branding, it is insufficient on its own to make the brand a strong one.

It is unfortunate that many companies believe (or are sometimes led to believe) that a new "corporate identity" in the form of a new logo, new corporate colors, improved retail-outlet design, a new slogan or tag line, or even a new name or abbreviation of the old name, can transform the company into a vibrant force with a grand image. When this happens—and it does—millions of dollars can be wasted, as little thought is given to whether such an overhaul will improve customer experience or perception of the company, thereby improving reputation and image. In other words, there is no real brand strategy; a superficial change in corporate identity alone does not constitute brand strategy.

Still, names and logos are important, especially when building an international brand. For example, disastrous mistakes can easily be made with names when venturing into new territory. Even experienced brand builders slip up. In the 1920s, Coca-Cola entered the Chinese market with the name (literally spelt), "kou-ke-kou-la." Unfortunately, this meant in Chinese (depending on the translation) "a thirsty mouth and full of candle wax" or "bite the wax tadpole." The Chinese name was subsequently changed to "ke-kou-ke-le," meaning "a joyful taste and happiness" or "happiness in the mouth." This change provided Coca-Cola with yet another resounding success story. Research is, therefore, a must before launching anything of a visual nature, especially a name, to the public in any country.

There is an enormous number of ways by which companies arrive at brand names. But, in all cases a few guidelines should not be ignored. Names should be:

- simple to spell
- easy to pronounce
- unusual and distinctive
- easy to recall
- protectable e.g. by trademark
- universally acceptable

This is a tall order; not even the Nike brand name is accepted in every country. But, every effort must be made to satisfy all the aforementioned requisites.

An interesting example of product naming is the branding of a particular French wine in Asia. In Asia, as wine consumers constitute a minority of the population, wine is not a mass-market seller. Regarded as an elite product with many varieties, French wines have names that are difficult to pronounce, and most people cannot distinguish one chateau's product from another, thus creating confusion. One company decided to cut through this confusion and developed a mass-market product. Its strategy to achieve this was by branding an acceptable French wine with a name that is easily recognizable in any type of outlet, whether a hotel, bar, restaurant, shop, or supermarket. The company's view was that the only way to remove the mystique of wines and raise demand from consumers who know little about them was by branding them. And so, the company did this with a simple, memorable, and recognizable name—*Malesan*. To raise brand-name awareness, a varied media plan was used, which included posters, billboards, and a television commercial. The name actually means nothing, but in Asia the sales response has so far been strong. The company says the branding has given the product meaning to the consumer.

Is a brand a product?

Some people believe that "brand" is just another word for a product. But, basic products marketed simply as products, do not become legends. It is the more intangible aspects, of value and emotional associations, that wrap around the product to make it something special. When people think of a product or service, they usually think of the attributes and features, and the practical benefits that the product or service will bring to consumers. But, when they think of a brand, they think beyond this and in a totally different way, because branding adds an emotional dimension to the product-customer relationship. The main aspect that makes brands special is personality. Before we examine brand personality (in Chapter 2), what it means to people, and how to build it, it is important to establish basics of branding in relation to the people's needs.

From product to brand: Basic brand anatomy

Branding is essentially based on the principle of satisfying the needs of consumers. But, people have various needs, some of which can be very emotionally based. Also, people do not always act rationally. In order to decide how to build a brand, a framework that encompasses these different needs must be built. It is interesting to start from the most basic product or service, and analyze the range of the needs that might be satisfied by it.

The basic composition of successfully branded products contains two basic constituents, namely, features and attributes, and emotional benefits. The first is common to all products, but the second is associated with brands. These elements tend to be driven by different sets of needs.

Features, attributes, and related practical benefits

These are the main components of a product, service, or company that is going to be branded. In the case of a company, they could be the size, business focus (i.e. what a company does), or sales organization of the firm. For a service, they could include the applicable terms and conditions, speed of delivery, etc. For a product, they could be physical or technical specifications. These features or attributes satisfy functional needs, and are usually not enough to distinguish a brand from its competition. This does not preclude, however, that if a product is new, there may be an element of uniqueness when it first enters the market. Because they are functionally driven, features and attributes are basically rational by nature, that is, they appeal to a person's logical way of thinking and of making comparisons.

Features and attributes have benefits associated with them, in terms of how they will satisfy the rational needs and wants of consumers, and there is a difference between needs and wants. For example, I might need some food to eat, but I want to eat a steak. Features and attributes satisfy rational needs: for example, the fluoride component of toothpaste helps prevent tooth decay. Meaningful features and attributes are essential as a pre-condition of entry into the market, because if a product or service does not satisfy the basic needs and wants of consumers, it will fail. Features and attributes are also relative as consumers compare them with those offered by competitors But, it is the benefits that satisfy emotional needs of people that are at the heart of some of the world's most spectacular brand building.

Emotional benefits

Consumers never really understand all the features and attributes that products and services have, unlike the companies that produce them. They do, however, know that they prefer some brands to others. This brand preference tends to stem from the emotional needs that people have. The secret to branding is in adding value, especially psychological value, to products, services, and companies in the form of intangible benefits—the emotional associations, beliefs, values, and feelings that people relate to the brand. It is this aspect of the product or service, and not the features and attributes, that can strongly distinguish in people's

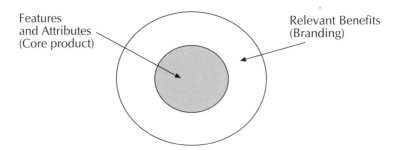

Figure 2: Basic brand structure: Product-centered.

minds one brand from another. This can be achieved by building a strong identity or personality for the brand, and strategically positioning it in the minds of the target audience. This is not an easy or quick process, but it is absolutely vital to brand success. For this reason, Chapter 2 looks at how to build brands in this way.

The three diagrams represent the alternative methods of brand building available.

Figure 2 typifies brands that emphasize functional characteristics. Companies using this approach concentrate on promoting their brands on the basis of the functional features and competencies the brands possess. An example of this would be the brands built by companies such as Sony Corporation. The features define the core product while quality, reliability, service aspects, and reputation form the relevant brand benefits.

An alternative approach to brand building is to center the brand around its core values, usually personality characteristics, and then build

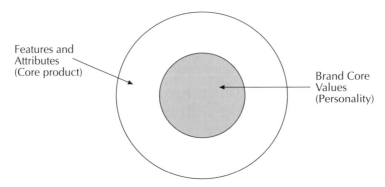

Figure 3: Basic brand structure: Values- and personality-centered.

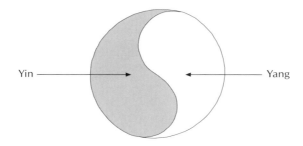

Figure 4: Basic brand structure: The *Yin–Yang* model,

product (service or company) features, attributes, benefits or imagery around this, as illustrated in Figure 3. Companies using this approach concentrate on personality, matching the brand's personality to those of the consumers, or giving the brand a personality that would attract people to it. An example of this brand structure would be brands built by companies like Philip Morris. Marlboro, for example, has strength and independence as its core values, and ways of expressing these via product communications and brand imagery would be the surround.

Of particular interest to Asian brands is the *Yin–Yang* model in Figure 4, which differs only slightly from the value-centered model, emphasizing the two sides of the branding equation well. This model states that brand success depends on both the rational and emotional sides of the brand, and that both are necessary, yet must work in harmony. So, if the *yin* represents the rational (with brand attributes such as quality, reliability), then there must be a balance of emotional attributes (such as freedom, friendliness), the *yang*. The *Yin–Yang* model suggests that the balance can be altered depending on the situation, which makes it valuable for brand communications. The TAG Heuer case study in Chapter 9 illustrates rational and emotional brand values.

CAN ANYTHING BE BRANDED?

We are all familiar with branded products like Kit Kat, companies like Sony Corporation, and services like FedEx, but we often forget that many other things can be branded too, such as entertainers, politicians, events, destinations and places, and even nations. The principles remain the same.

Entertainers and celebrities are often the result of skillful branding. Michael Jordan, Tiger Woods, Mariah Carey, Jay Leno, Jackie Chan, and others are good examples of what the power of branding can achieve. Star Trek is more than just an ongoing space-fantasy soap opera, it is a brand with millions of constantly satisfied customers (viewers). Star Trek memorabilia sales chalk up millions, and conventions and associated events abound. Actors starring in the series come and go, but the Star Trek brand lives on. The X-Files is a similar entertainment brand. Disneyland has become the top destination on practically every family's wish-list. Events like the Football World Cup and the Super Bowl attract billions of television viewers. The Manchester United Football Club has been so successful in branding itself that it has become a target for acquisition. It is setting up a chain of amusement parks in Asia called "Theatre of Dreams" to cater to its millions of fans (an estimated 20 million in China alone), having already established retail outlets in some Asian countries.

Politicians are also good examples of branding. Margaret Thatcher changed her brand image totally prior to getting elected as British prime minister, and George Bush's 1988 presidential election campaign was an astonishing success with the change in his image from a low positive-negative ratio of around 40% to a much improved and winning result of 60%. Countries are also using the techniques of branding to change perceptions. For example, Taiwan is carrying out a long-term campaign aimed at changing business people's perceptions of its identity to a more high-tech image. As can be seen from the above examples, anything or anyone can be branded.

The success of branding depends to a certain extent on the quality of the product, service, or person. Many singers and politicians, for instance, possess certain abilities, but it is the perceived image others have of them that wins the day for them and enhances their value. However, branding should not be used as a substitute for poor quality or inferior performance. Allowing situations like this to slip through can result in sales slipping too, as Jaguar found out in the 1970s, when it let its product quality drop to unprecedented depths. So, when building a brand, it is important to remember that the product or service on offer must be seen to be at least as good as that the competition. In the 21st century, however, quality and performance levels, of competing products and services especially, will be on par with each other. It will, therefore, require more than these two factors to make a product or service appear greatly superior to its competition. It is branding that creates lasting differentiation, and in many cases, legendary success. In order to understand how branding achieves this, we have to first recognize what it is about brands that causes people to prefer them to ordinary products.

WHY DO CONSUMERS LIKE BRANDS?

People are always talking about brands. Even young children discuss their favorite brands. Why then do the majority of consumers prefer to buy branded products and services as opposed to commodity-type goods and services? There are several reasons for this.

Brands generate choice

Brands provide consumers with a means of choice. The mere existence of brand names makes it easier to differentiate one product from another. Over the years, the power of the consumer in terms of knowledge and rights has risen while the broadening range of brands facilitates the freedom of choice, which is valued so highly. Customers have better knowledge of branded products and services than they do of commodity-types. As such, customers are able to choose easily from among branded products and services than unbranded, unfamiliar, and similar offerings.

Brands simplify decisions

First, brands make shopping easier because branded packaging facilitates quick recognition of a product. Living in a fast-paced world, people are constantly looking for ways to make their lives less frustrating. Being able to home in on a favorite brand saves time and effort.

Second, branding often helps arriving at a purchase decision more quickly. This aspect is particularly important to people who are buying technical products, as they do not always understand all the specifications and jargon fired at them by sales staff and promotional leaflets. Furthermore, when products from various manufacturers are technically indistinguishable, it is the brand name that offers comfort and simplicity. Intel is a good example here.

Brands offer quality assurance and reduce risk

When customers repeatedly buy a certain brand, they quickly get a feel for the quality and value for money they can expect from that brand. For example, stepping into a Kentucky Fried Chicken (KFC) outlet anywhere in the world, one knows precisely the quality of food to expect. This expectation (associated with a brand) helps a customer avoid the risk associated with buying untried products and services. Most customers are risk-averse and avoid the unknown, but brands offer them security and reduce worry and fear. In addition, if a brand fails to live up to its acceptable level of quality, customers have recourse to the manufacturer. Companies, as a result, try harder to maintain quality standards and their reputations.

Brands help self-expression

An important reason why most people prefer brands is that brands provide an avenue for self-expression. When asked why the company had introduced computers available in many colors, Steve Jobs of Apple Computer replied that people do not care so much about megabytes and gigabytes, but instead want to express themselves through the color of their computers. Such psychological need is often at the heart of a purchase decision because brands become the means through which people can express their personality, aspirations, and achievements. By using or wearing a particular brand, customers can express something about themselves that normally they might not be able to or willing to do.

In Asia, it is common to find successful people expressing their wealth or success through their Mercedes-Benz cars or Rolex watches. An advertisement in a Singapore newspaper by a Mercedes-Benz distributor featured a picture of an E-class model with the tag line: Make a statement, without saying a word. Consumers buy expensive and prestigious brands of goods because possession of these outward expressions of success differentiates them from other people, and gives them the opportunity to stand out from the crowd. Prestige brands are world famous, and there is no shortage of people waiting to buy them.

Further explanation of how brands generate this kind of appeal is given in Chapter 2.

Brands offer friendship and pleasure

Brands offer psychological benefits that far outweigh the practical benefits of the product. In some cases, consumers form strong associations with a brand, leading to friendship and even dependency. The value of logos and names increases as brand association becomes more indelible in the psyche of consumers. Logos and names become triggers that, upon recognition, recall memories and feelings associated with the brand. Brands, therefore, can generate intense emotion and pleasure. This, too, is discussed in greater detail in the next chapter, where the psychology and techniques of brand building are also outlined.

THE DIFFERENCE BETWEEN BRAND IDENTITY AND BRAND IMAGE

The terms brand identity and brand image are sometimes confused with each other, leading to errors of judgment in marketing and brand building. The result is often a credibility gap that damages the reputation of a business—its image.

Brand identity

Many Asian companies are familiar with the term "brand image," but the term is used very loosely. The term "brand identity" is rarely used though, and is generally not understood. This leads to misunderstanding about the very nature of branding.

One of the key activities in branding is the creation of an identity for a product, service, or company—to give it personality. With entertainers, sports celebrities, or politicians, the "raw material" for the intended identity already exists. But, with non-human subjects, it may initially appear to be more difficult to achieve. A person's identity is reflected in his/her appearance, actions, and behavior. The way a person dresses, speaks, acts, or moves, indicates whether he/she is trustworthy, creative, friendly, etc. The challenge in branding a non-human subject is to evoke the personality traits, and it can be done. A product, for example, can be physically dressed differently (packaging), speak differently, (through the tone used in commercials), and have other specific characteristics such as reliability. The sum total is its identity— it is the whole of what is being offered. As with people, so too with places, countries, products, services and companies—their identity involves depth, substance, character, performance, and other such qualities.

The aim of providing brands with identities (including their own names) is to get people to like them and see them as being unique in some way. By doing so, branding will succeed in generating the kind of brand image desired. When determining what this desired brand image should be, never overlook that, in addition to the basic expectations created, every customer hopes for personal recognition and attention beyond the normal acceptable standards, and to be associated with something special.

Brand image

The importance of image

In today's markets, most companies provide similar products and services. Fundamentally, these markets are commodity markets driven by prime needs and minimum standards of service. When customers consider such factors, some products and services will meet their requirements. How do customers differentiate them? When the basic qualifying factors are in place and the consumer is considering all the available options, brand image resoundingly comes into play—company or product imaging becomes fundamental to the decision. Image is highly important to companies in Asia, where essentially collectivist cultures prevail in every country and image represents "face" as well as quality.

Brand identity should drive brand image

Although image is important, it is identity that should drive the brand. The identity or personality of the brand gives it consistency and longevity. Many companies are tempted by results of brand-image research to change their brand's identity. But, it is identity and the values upon which the identity is based that define the brand. Brand image is how the brand is seen, but this is only a point of comparison against the identity. Companies must be prepared to change the image, not the identity, if the two do not match. Guardianship of brand identity is, therefore, essential.

Image is the market's summation of the complete product—the way it perceives the total experience, brand against brand. Largely, it is the thrust, tone, and manner of a company's communications, and the consumer's experience with the brand that builds its image. Brand image should reflect and express the brand personality.

A brand's image, however, may not be the same as the identity we would like the brand to have. Image is a product of people's perceptions, that is, the way in which people think about or even imagine something to be. There is a real danger in assuming that the image we want people to have of our brand will be the same as the identity we are trying to project, as this might not always be the case. For instance, people might view a company as dull and unexciting when it is actually trying to appear lively. Or a company's new headquarters may appear far too opulent when the company is actually trying to look prudent. This difference between identity and image is called a "perception gap," and is to be avoided at all costs. Unfortunately, it is a common weakness found in many companies. There are many instances in Asian countries of companies claiming to have impeccable service standards, but failing to translate this service into customer experience. So, remember that when building a brand, great care must be taken to insure that the brand image matches its identity. The golden rule is: Do not promise what you cannot deliver.

Some companies set goals for their brand identity in terms of the desired image they would like the brand to have. One company has written down typical desired consumer responses to define what these perceptions mean, for instance:

• Service-oriented: "It's easy to do business with Company X because its service and the way it does business are second to none."

By spelling out its brand values to its employees, and including sample situations that staff might come across with customers, the company is helping all its staff take responsibility for managing the brand, and for developing a brand culture that delivers on the promises made. Consequently, this company has developed a highly successful corporate brand. But, branding can be accomplished at various levels.

LEVELS OF BRANDING

There are several branding strategies that a company can choose to determine the focus of the brand it is creating and developing. The basis for the choice of strategy boils down to a central issue, for whatever reason, which is how prominent should the company brand name be in relation to the product or service brand name. The decision has implications for not just marketing communications, but also the development of the whole relationship between the brand and its customers.

The principal four levels of branding or brand strategies companies can opt for are:

• product branding
• product-line branding
• product-range branding
• corporate branding

Product branding

Product branding lies at one end of the brand-strategy spectrum. It entails giving each individual product an exclusive brand name, with the company name either totally or virtually absent. Companies such as Procter & Gamble are famous for product branding, for example, with Tide washing powder.

This strategy allows the brand to have unique values, personality, identity, and positioning. As a consequence, this approach implies that every new product the company brings on to the market, is a new brand and can be positioned precisely for a specific market segment. This makes it easier for the company to evaluate brand performance and worth, and allows better resource-allocation decisions. A potential problem is that product cannibalization can occur if consumers cannot differentiate clearly among product brands, that is, if the product positioning is not clear. Another disadvantage of this strategy is that every product brand requires its own advertising and promotion budget, and is totally self-supporting, with little or no brand name assistance or assurance from the parent.

Product-line branding

In this approach, products appear under the same brand name and possess the same basic identity, but with slightly different competencies; for example, a line of hair shampoos like Follow Me, that has different benefits. The brand line comes under the hair-care category, but the different line extensions cover complementary applications of essentially the same product. Clearly, the various products remain very close to the initial brand concept. Economies of scale in advertising and promotion are a feature in this strategy, and each new line extension strengthens the positioning of the brand and, therefore, its image. The line helps defend the category from predatory attack. In this way, individual product brands move across to line brands as companies find ways of extending the brand to different customer groups or segments.

Product-range branding

Product-range brand strategy is one where a number of products or services in a broad category are grouped together under one brand name and promoted with one basic identity. Unlike line-branded products (mentioned in the earlier section), these range-branded products carry out basically the same functions, but at different performance levels. Examples of such products include the various cars in the Mercedes S-, E-, C- and A-class, and Intel's Pentium and Celeron ranges of microprocessors. A single brand name allows some economies of scale in advertising and promotion, as the products tend to carry the same overall brand values and positioning.

Corporate branding

There are basically two approaches to corporate branding. One is the decision a company takes to promote its name as the main brand name, sometimes referred to as monolithic or umbrella branding. In this approach, the product or service offered is not branded individually or as strongly as the corporate brand. The aim is to leverage the corporate identity and image. Companies with powerful images, such as IBM and Virgin, use this branding method. Akio Morita, the founder of Sony Corporation, expressed well the rationale for corporate branding when he said: "I have always believed that the company name is the life of an enterprise. It carries responsibility and guarantees the quality of the product."

Many Asian companies have taken this route because the commitment and longevity of the company are judged to be of great importance in their countries.

The need to satisfy the consumers' concerns about credibility and quality is an important reason why the second approach to corporate branding is becoming popular. In this approach, the product brand name has a high profile, but is endorsed by the parent company, which gives the product a stamp of quality and credibility. The product brand is self-supporting in practically every respect, but retains the assurance of the corporate brand endorsement. This brand strategy is sometimes referred to as house or endorsement branding.

It is a popular form of branding used by well-known multinational companies such as Nestlé. With a multitude of brands in its portfolio, Nestlé sometimes needs to give its products the protection and guarantee of performance to make them profitable in highly competitive categories. New products especially can find it very difficult to break into mature markets without the endorsement of a strong and credible corporate parental brand name. This type of corporate branding is also very appropriate to those companies engaged in service industries, as their products are more intangible in nature. When consumers cannot see the product, the company name helps give them an assurance of quality, heritage, and authenticity.

HOW DOES BRANDING FIT INTO CORPORATE STRATEGY?

Branding has made marketing more strategic than it was two decades ago. The marketing mix is now seen more as an arsenal of tactical weapons, with the brands playing the big guns. Top brands have their own vision, mission, financial and marketing objectives, and a whole array of strategies to achieve these ambitions. The top brands are run as corporate entities in their own right, right down to their profitability and equity valuation. The introductory chapter mentioned the huge rewards that can be achieved by companies possessing strong international and global brands. In some cases, the brand is the company and the company is the brand. From this viewpoint, brands are a vital part of corporate strategy.

Much has been said about globalization and competing in a borderless world with international goods and services both in the domestic and international markets. It is hastily assumed that the competition will be between products—judged on quality, service, supply. In fact, Asian goods, still viewed and promoted as products, will come up against not just other products but established brands.

For Asian companies, the branding route is undoubtedly the one to travel. Companies are unlikely to attain world-class financial performance or global recognition without building at least one strong brand, whether corporate or product. Branding is strategic and should be a permanent item on boardroom agendas.

Company visions and missions are often defined, and strategies are put in place to help achieve them. Brand and corporate strategies are extremely close. However, it is rare for Asian companies to have brand-strategy blueprints for either corporate or product brands, or clear brand platforms upon which such blueprints can be based. A strong brand platform (the way in which a brand is positioned and given personality) becomes the raw material for product development and differentiation meaningful to the consumer. A clear brand-strategy blueprint provides the foundation for image development—a "glue" that binds all strategic activities in a co-ordinated and synergistic way. Internally, a strong, well-defined brand-strategy blueprint will assist employee understanding of the company's strategic marketing objectives and their roles in achieving these objectives, thus boosting motivation, purpose, pace, and productivity. Externally, brand communications will inform the world of the company's corporate and brand values, achievements, and why they are different and better. A strong and well-executed brand-strategy blueprint is fundamental to the achievement of the company's vision, and will impact strongly on the bottom line. Given the current economic downturn in Asia, affecting all industries, an excellent window of opportunity now exists for companies to develop their brand strategies for the future. More information on brand-strategy blueprints is given in Chapter 2.

Branding in sports is big business. The first case study shows how the New Zealand rugby team has tried to change its brand image by changing its brand personality. Even at the team level, branding works and New Zealand is currently the most popular rugby team in the world.

From sports to fashion, the Padini Holdings case study highlights how top management passion for its brands is translated into market success. The fashion industry is a difficult one to succeed in, and risks have to be taken. But, Padini has minimized the risks by really understanding what customers want.

The third case study is about branding a country. Anything can be branded, and Britain in Malaysia was a highly successful branding exercise, changing market perceptions and image, resulting in business success.

Case Study 1

THE NEW ZEALAND RUGBY TEAM
The All Blacks work hard
to establish a new brand personality

The New Zealand rugby team is a business, especially since professionalism in sport spread to the Rugby Union. The team has stakeholders who are given a return on their investment, and the product is in the hands of the players. As a result, the market environment has changed, and with it comes customer expectations. The profile of the game in general has risen, and rugby teams are now becoming conscious of the fact that their image can impact business revenues significantly.

Manager John Hart said how much his New Zealand rugby team now realizes "the value of image and the power of marketing." All Blacks is the brand name of the New Zealand rugby team. In the past, the team had not enjoyed a good image despite consistently winning more games than any other international team. According to the All Blacks' management, the team was viewed as cold, remote, stern, unforgiving, and reticent. People perceived the team to be arrogant and full of themselves, and their behavior on and off the field tended to reinforce this unfavorable perception. This image of invincibility helped the All Blacks win many games when the odds were down and the physical skills of both the team and their opponents were evenly matched, purely through psychological means.

But this is changing. The All Blacks are conscious that they have a brand that they intend to market effectively. They realize that the development of a brand in the new business of rugby involves more than scoring higher points than the opposition—it is about being admired. The All Blacks have made the decision to send a clear signal about their team and their sport, and to change the world's perceptions of them, all towards creating a better image. This principally involved working hard to bring about a personality change for the brand. It was based on making themselves more approachable and friendly; being admired, loved and envied; and being professional and individualistic. No code of conduct or personality statement was laid down, but the team culture had to change.

To effect this change, players were encouraged to express themselves as individuals on and off the field, but within the confines of the All Blacks tradition of no one man being greater than the team. Even walking about town was encouraged unlike before. Every team member was made aware of the image he should be projecting. As their inspiring former captain, Sean Fitzpatrick, said: "We are always very aware to promote our brand in our behavior and presentation, individually and as a group." Professionalism on and off the field was also emphasized. The new personality also encompasses humility, as Fitzpatrick states: "We have always strove to improve and be better. We don"t think of ourselves as being great."

Visually, the team also tries to project a consistent brand identity, rejecting photography shoots that do not reflect the brand or result in the right image. It was a determined effort by all who joined the business, not just the players.

The result is that the All Blacks are still one of the top teams in the world of rugby, and are now gaining share of heart as well as share of mind.

Brand strengths: professionalism, consistency, establishing brand personality and culture.
Source: *Rugby World*

Case Study 2

PADINI HOLDINGS
Creating and managing brands in a fast-changing market

Padini Holdings is a fast-growing company, and you might be forgiven for thinking that it is of Italian origin—it is Malaysian. Yong Pang Chaun founded the company in 1971 and gave it an Italian-sounding name—appropriate for the fashion world— that would help overcome the difficulties associated with a country of origin not thought of as the home of quality fashion goods.

Since its founding, Padini Holdings has become tremendously successful, becoming a listed company in early 1998. Yong and his talented young management team have a passion for their business and their brands, all of which have become famous national names. The key to Padini Holdings' success has been its skill in creating and managing several brands, aimed mainly at younger people, without falling into the trap of product cannibalization. It is also based on a sound strategic positioning. The business philosophy is to offer a unique combination of value for money and excitement, giving all customers the opportunity to experience the thrill of global fashion in an affordable way.

The brands

The company and its first brand shared the same name, Padini, but since then, the company has moved away from corporate branding towards product branding. Padini, the original brand intended for men, offers younger professionals businessman classic shirts and pants, while the brand Padini Authentics casual wear offers the same market segment. The brand Seed targets young-minded, fashion-conscious males and females who like modern and trendy clothes. The brand also has a similar clothing range for the children of this market segment.

Miki Kids is a well-established brand that offers colorful clothing for children, and this line has been extended with Miki Mom. Rope is a brand offering work outfits for career women, and Vincci is a range of complementary shoes and accessories. P & Co caters to teenagers and young adults with exciting and fashionable clothing that is more casual and less expensive than Seed. The latest brand addition is PDI, targeted at a wide range of customers with its easy styles, basic items, and low prices.

The market segmentation has been carefully researched. Padini Holdings looks for gaps in the market and, after carrying out customer research to build a composite picture of the "prototypical" consumer, taking into account global fashion trends, analyzing competitor offerings, and gearing up for production, it positions its brands appropriately. This clear definition of its targets market minimizes error.

Risk-taking is essential

Errors, however, are an unavoidable part of the fashion-based business. The complexity of managing several brands in competitive fashion markets is signified by the fact that Padini Holdings introduces over 10,000 product lines each year. Not all succeed, and constant vigilance is necessary to spot the lines that are doing well, tapering off, or are not selling. This means that speed of responding to the market place is vital for success, and all the company's resources support this. Of course, not all products are huge successes, but failure to respond quickly means missing out on the fast-moving market trends. The answer to this dilemma is very clear to Yong, who says: "There is no future in retail if you are not prepared to take risks, make mistakes, and learn from them. You must be receptive and open, seizing every opportunity."

The Future: Taking a brand regionally

Powerful international brands always start off success with in their home markets. So, what does the future hold for Padini Holdings? What are the plans Padini Holdings has for establishing its brands internationally? Wisely, it is proposing a regional step first with the brand that has the most potential— Seed. This brand could be a regional market leader within three to five years, but the company recognizes the difficulties involved.

The principal challenge is to change current market perception of the brand being local rather than international. But, the management team takes a long-term view, and realizes that as the fashion market becomes more open and competitive in manufacturing and marketing, parity will be the order of the day. And, when everything is equal, companies will face a war of the brands. It is then that image becomes the differentiator.

To meet this challenge, the company has already started investing more in the brand, with increased advertising and promotion expenditure, and the opening of a bright new flagship store in a prestigious location. It is also preparing to face other strategic problems that lie ahead. For instance, merchandising, advertising, and promotion will have to become more sophisticated, and quality will have to reach even higher standards. Distribution channels will have to be restructured. It will become mandatory only to move product through outlets that present the brand with the required style, consistency, and appropriateness. Yong and his team are prepared to do this, in addition to sacrificing a share of market for a share of mind. Their passion and belief in the brand is unshakable.

Padini Holdings does not underestimate the task it has set itself—but it has a dream and is determined to see it come true.

Brand strengths: brand passion, understanding of market segments, speed of response, strategic positioning,

Case Study 3

BRANDING A COUNTRY
Britain in Malaysia—Just between friends

An assortment of British activity was scheduled in 1998 which, coupled with Malaysia's own plans, presented an opportunity for Britain to reinforce its commitment to Malaysia and the strength of the partnership. Throughout 1998, the British High Commission, together with the British-Malaysian Industry and Trade Association, The British Tourist Authority, The British Council, British Airways, and the North West Arts Board, ran a consolidated and co-ordinated theme-campaign, which brought together under one umbrella all the individual activities organized by these groups, and other British-related events.

A professional branding approach was adopted to present a single identity of "Britain in Malaysia." The first step towards achieving this was to establish a set of core brand values and a brand personality, which would be stressed throughout the campaign and beyond. These core values (namely, four personality characteristics) were defined carefully to insure total commitment from all participating organizations. The target audiences were identified, and a brand positioning statement, which was capable of being interpreted for many different market segments, was agreed upon. A professionally designed logo was developed to reflect the new consolidated personality. The positioning statement included a series of key messages created for each target audience.

Four core values were chosen to portray Britain, British companies, and British products and services in a way very different to how they were being perceived by the target Malaysian audience and in Asia in general. The four core values (brand personality characteristics) were:

- innovativeness
- dependability
- professionalism
- stylishness

These four values were defined carefully. They had to be believable, credible, and capable of being demonstrated during the campaign. Some examples of the key messages that were to be projected through them were:

- innovativeness—state of the art technology, creativity in ideas, flexibility in structures and business activity

- dependability—long-term historical relationship between the two countries, long-term commitment, familiarity with systems and language

- professionalism—trustworthiness and reliability, performing to high standards, quality of training and education

- stylishness—trendsetting, fun, excellence, elegance, heritage

These personality characteristics were summarized in a short positioning statement (for internal briefing purposes only) which said: "To support Malaysia in achieving its vision, Britain is your dependable and innovative partner in Europe, committed to sharing world-class excellence, skills, and technology." A tag line "Just Between Friends" was introduced to summarize the brand positioning.

During the campaign year, it was important to insure that everyone concerned was briefed on the brand, the reasons for its creation, and its personality. This applied not just to the British institutions and companies incumbent in Malaysia, but also to all the organizers and sponsors of every event in the campaign. Briefing kits were produced, and all event organizers were encouraged to incorporate the brand values, logo, and tag line in their advertising and promotional activities. In fact, the use of the logo was mandatory for all who wished to be a part of the campaign. In this way, every visitor, from trade mission members to Whitehall officials, could marry their messages to the overall "Britain in Malaysia" campaign.

As the then High Commissioner British to Malaysia, David Moss, said at the launch of the campaign: "We have, over the past months, been developing a strategy to promote the campaign. We have sought expert advice and have come up with a set of values which we believe suitably stress why Britain is better and unique. We have designed a logo and thought up a tag line to tie in with and promote these values... These ambitious goals equate to a major program of arts, educational, and trade-related events. If presented professionally and backed by a consistent message from all those in the British community, they will significantly raise the profile and image of Britain in Malaysia."

The whole campaign was a resounding success, with more people attending events than was expected. For example, the "U.K. Today" exhibition alone—just one event in the campaign —attracted 49,000 visitors, tenfold more than expected. The "franchising" of the logo helped the campaign to produce a cascading effect, putting across the messages at different levels to a wide cross-section of society.

With reference to the future, the High Commissioner said: "The values we have adopted will remain relevant well beyond 1998. As such, we shall be able to build on them in years to come to present an even stronger image of Britain in Malaysia. And as any successful company will testify, the application of a set of key values in a consistent year-on-year fashion has proved to be the best investment in image building that they can make. By consistently stressing why Britain is different and better through the values we have identified, we shall provide the strategic platform for the successful presentation of all British activity in Malaysia."

The brand values and personality have remained relevant beyond 1998, and are continuing to be a driving force in the development of an even stronger image of Britain in Malaysia.

2

How Brands Are Built

In this chapter, we will look at how world-class companies build their brands. The techniques can be implemented by any organization, but there must be a disciplined effort by all within the organization to insure that the core elements of the brand are applied with total consistency.

THE PSYCHOLOGY OF BRANDING

Branding relies on the understanding of psychology—how people think and how they consequently behave. Much of our understanding of how branding and brand communications work stems from the Swiss psychologist, Carl Jung. In his work, Jung referred to four distinct functions of the mind, namely:

- thought
- feeling
- sensation
- intuition

Marketeers have found that making a brand appeal to these four mental functions can give it a competitive advantage.

Thought

The thinking part of the mind concerns rationality and logic, often referred to as left-brain activities. The left brain is concerned totally with analysis, deduction, numeracy, and other logical procedures. Rationality and logic can be powerful persuaders, and can influence buying behavior because they provide reasons why a certain course of action should be taken. This understanding of the brain function has resulted in brands being presented rationally to consumers. For example, a toothpaste with fluoride helps prevent tooth decay, which is a good reason to buy it. Projecting rationality and reason into brand communications can be useful. However, it is not the only way in which minds can be influenced.

Feeling

Feeling is also another powerful influence on human behavior, and can be stimulated by advertising and promotional activities. Feeling belongs to the right brain, which is concerned with emotions, happiness, fear, anger, sadness, and love. For example, images of a puppy happily playing with toilet tissue or of a sad, undernourished child can evoke emotional feelings in almost everyone. Most brand managers now agree that building a strong brand that appeals to consumer feelings and emotions is essential, wherever possible. This can be accomplished largely by building a personality into the brand.

Sensation

Sensation, as the word suggests, concerns the senses of touch, taste, sound, smell, and sight. It is a right-brain function. Again, brand communications can stimulate desire by appealing to any one or more of these mental sensory processes. As the senses are connected to feelings and emotions, they can be powerful persuaders. For instance, music from a past era can evoke nostalgia. The Hovis brand of bread achieved a great marketing success by appealing to the sensory function in a famous television commercial. Shot using sepia-type photography, the commercial showed a small boy, dressed in pre-war clothing, climbing a steep cobblestone hill, packed on either side with old-fashioned back-to-back houses, and bringing the loaf of bread back to his home. Nostalgic brass band music played as he walked. Brands can evoke lasting memories.

Companies such as Chanel, Lancôme, and Clinique are using a recent different and exciting development that appeals to consumers' senses through placing fragrant strips in magazines. As brand integrity has to be maintained, product quality must be unassailable, and the strips must smell exactly like the brand promoted. This makes the technology complex, but the results have evidently been fantastic. Statistics for this type of promotion show that 68% of readers buy the product after smelling a fragrance in a magazine. Each advertisement costs only an additional 3.5 US cents per page.

Intuition

Intuition is yet another right-brain function. Intuition defies logic and rationality, and is often acted out in impulsive behavior. Statements like: "I just knew it was the right thing to say" or "I don't know why I bought it—I just knew it was for me," are typical examples of people trying to justify intuitive and spontaneous behavior. Marketeers latch on to the intuitive process by studying the lifestyles and interests of consumers, analyzing when and how customers decide to buy.

An understanding of all four functions of the mind is essential to those wishing to build brands because these functions constitute the personality of every individual. Brand builders have learnt much about personality, and have cleverly adopted much of this knowledge into brand strategies in an effort to get really close to customers and form deep, lasting relationships with them. As a natural corollary, one of the key skills in branding is to construct personalities for products, companies, and even countries. Brand personality is one of the two major elements involved in brand building; the other is strategic positioning. Together, they form the basic platform necessary for any company to develop a brand-strategy blueprint.

THE NEED FOR A BRAND-STRATEGY BLUEPRINT

In Chapter 1, we saw that a brand-strategy blueprint was posited as vital to achieving corporate vision and image. This concerns developing in the longer term a brand to help fulfill the corporate or brand vision, and involves examining the most productive areas of development for the immediate term. Usually, the resulting blueprint follows a line of logic through situations, trends, challenges, recommendations, a brand-strategy summary, and the steps to be taken in the future. It is normal for companies to have embarked on many brand-related activities, most of which are tactical such as promotional campaigns, and these would have contributed to the prevailing image of the brand. In Asian companies, however, it is rare to find a document that sets out the vision, values, personality, and positioning for the brand, together with the implications and guidelines for visual and product differentiation, brand culture and architecture, and other aspects of longer-term brand strategy. These are essential components of what can be called a strategic brand blueprint.

In order to draw up a strategic brand blueprint, a brand audit has first to be carried out to assess the identity of the brand and its current equity, i.e. its strengths. The objective is to analyze all brand-related knowledge and activities, and to create a strategic focus, with practical examples showing options for progress. The most important part of a brand-strategy blueprint is the development of the strategic brand platform. This platform is the focus of this chapter and a major part of the book. If the platform is not developed correctly, then a brand-strategy blueprint will have no basis. Consequently, the brand will develop in a haphazard fashion, possibly resulting in an uncontrollable image.

CREATING A STRATEGIC BRAND PLATFORM

Brands are made up of basic features, attributes, and consumer benefits. However, it is the brand's values, which consumers perceive as being unique and successful, that make a brand successful. A good brand has both a *yin* side and a *yang* side, as mentioned in Chapter 1. Both offer promises that appeal to consumers. On the *yin* side (comprising features, etc.), the promise tends to be based around quality and other tangible items. This is vital because all strong brands possess outstanding quality. On the *yang* side, the promise is usually something special—a set of associations or intangible benefits—that differentiates the brand from others. Building powerful brands is all about adding perceived value to a company, product, or service, so that each brand has a unique identity.

It is also about creating and developing the emotional associations that attract consumers, and this is best done by adding personality to the brand.

The development of a strategic brand platform, therefore, depends on careful selection, development and management of a brand personality, and proposed ownership of a specific and unique position in the minds of consumers. The consistency of appeal that world-class brands generate does not happen by accident. Companies achieve this by painstakingly applying all aspects of the marketing mix to a strategic brand platform that acts as a blueprint for action.

In selecting a strategic platform for its brand, the company must consider its readily available assets and choose a strategic communications pivot that:

- the market will recognize as real and supportable now
- the market finds attractive and meaningful now
- in a commodity market (which many markets are), provides a positive and meaningful point of difference
- represents a viable long-term position that will become increasingly attractive as time progresses
- can be tangibly underpinned by differentiating elements of product development

The most effective way to build a brand platform is by carefully thinking through and developing a brand personality and strategic position.

These two fundamental elements of brand building form the brand identity—the overall brand proposition. While companies continue to develop presence and its products, it is personality that can, and will, increasingly provide the unique point of difference. Just as with human beings, presence alone is not enough. A person can be present in any given situation without making any impact or attracting notice. It is personality that defines his/her individuality—the ability to stand out in a crowd. Substitute crowd with the market place inundated with competing products. Strategic positions are often created either deliberately or by default. But the part that is often overlooked is the development of a unique personality of great appeal to consumers. Both are, of course, important. The next section deals with brand personality. Strategic positioning will be dealt with in depth in Chapter 4.

WHY BRAND PERSONALITY?

It is the personality of a brand that can appeal to the four functions of the mind. For example, people make judgments about products and companies in personality terms. They might say, "I don't *think* that company is very friendly," "I *feel* uneasy when I go into that branch," "I just know that salesmen is not telling the truth about that product," or "That offer doesn't smell right to me." Their minds work in a personality driven way. Given that this is true, how then can a company create a personality for its product or for itself? The answer lies in the choice and application of personality values and characteristics.

Imagine a person as a brand. She may be around 28 years of age, with fair features, a small build, and be pleasant-looking. These would be similar to a product's features. When you get to know her a little better, your relationship may deepen, and you will be able to trust her, enjoy her company, and even miss her a lot when she is not around. She is fun to be with and you are strongly attracted to her values and concerns. These are emotions similar to the associations that people develop with brand personalities. People, generally, like people. So, if a personality can be created for a brand, it will be easier to attract consumers to the brand. As brands grow, as do human relationships, it is the emotional dimension that tends to become dominant in loyalty. Personality grows brands by providing the emotional difference and experience.

Values and characteristics of brand personality

People's personalities are determined largely through the values and beliefs they have, and other personality characteristics they develop. An example of a value or belief is honesty. Many people believe in being honest in everything they do and say. An example of a characteristic is confidence. This is not a belief, but more a behavior. There are, of course, many values, beliefs, and characteristics that a person may have, but there are some that are particularly likable. It is to these likable values and characteristics that people are inevitably attracted. Examples include dependability, trustworthiness, honesty, reliability, friendliness, caring, and fun-loving.

There are about two hundred words that describe personality characteristics, and these can be used for incorporating personality into brands. To illustrate how people think in personality terms when making judgments about brands, here are the results of a consumer survey of how people feel about two companies. When asked the question: "If these two companies were people, how would you describe them?" Their replies were:

Company A	Company B
Sophisticated	Easygoing
Arrogant	Modest
Efficient	Helpful
Self-centered	Caring
Distant	Approachable
Disinterested	Interested

These two companies are actually competitors in a service industry. If you were asked which of these two companies you would like to be your friend, you would probably choose Company B, as did 95% of the respondents. It is not surprising that the service level of Company B can be a better experience for customers than that of Company A. It is also easy to conclude that if consumers consistently experience these differences between the two companies, then the brand image of Company B will be much better than that of Company A.

A further point of interest arising out of this research is that people tend to prefer brands that fit in with their self-concept. Everyone has views about themselves and how they would like to be seen by others. And they tend to like personalities that are similar to theirs or to those whom they admire. Thus, creating brands with personalities similar to those of a certain group of consumers will be an effective strategy. The closer the brand personality is to the consumer personality (or one which they admire or aspire to), the greater will be the willingness to buy the brand and the deeper the brand loyalty.

Creating brand personality

Whether a brand is a product or a company, the company has to decide what personality traits the brand is to have. There are various ways of creating brand personality. One way is to match the brand personality as closely as possible to that of the consumers or to a personality that they like. The process will be:

- define the target audience
- find out what they need, want, and like
- build a consumer personality profile
- create the product personality to match that profile

This type of approach is favored by companies such as Levi Strauss, which researches its target audience fastidiously. For Levi's the result is a master-brand personality that is:

- original
- masculine
- sexy
- youthful
- rebellious
- individual
- free
- American

A related product brand personality (for a specific customer group) such as Levi's 501 jeans includes traits of:

- romance
- sexual attractiveness
- rebelliousness
- physical prowess
- resourcefulness
- independence
- liking admiration

Both profiles appeal mostly to the emotional side of people's minds—to their feelings and sensory functions. This profiling approach aims at reinforcing the self-concept of the consumers and their aspirations. The approach is ideal for brands that adopt a market-niche strategy, and can be extremely successful if a market segment has a high degree of global homogeneity, as is the case with Levi's. The youth market is fairly consistent universally in its preferences, behaviors, and aspirations, although there are some cultural variations as detailed in the Levi's case study in Chapter 9.

With regards to building a corporate brand where the customer base is likely to be very broad, this profiling approach is not feasible. In corporate branding, companies can either identify behavioral strengths that they already have, or decide to build a brand based on personality characteristics that they would like to be seen as having. For example, if a company has established a new vision and mission, the typical issues to be dealt with include:

- what is the company's vision and mission?
- how does it impact the company's future identity?
- what behaviors does the company need to achieve these?
- what personality characteristics will facilitate these behaviors?

A mission that involves social responsibility, for instance, might necessitate a personality that has the characteristics of being responsible, caring, resourceful, friendly, and reliable.

If a company has a poor image, it might decide to try and change consumer perceptions by concentrating on projecting a more favorable and likable personality. For example, if a company is seen as aloof and self-centered, it may wish to focus on new characteristics of being caring and approachable.

There are other ways of determining brand personality characteristics, such as through staff consultation surveys, brainstorming, and so on. Some characteristics may be created by the company founder. However it is done, the chosen personality must be rigorously adhered to if it is to be effective. This will be discussed in a later section, Brand Guardianship, of this chapter.

Brand personality is long-term

Human personality changes only slowly over time, having been largely formed before the age of seven. Similarly, brand personality must evolve slowly, and not be subject to rapid or frequent changes. We think it very odd if our friends are unpredictable in their behavior, and in general, society views people with changing or alternative personalities, as manic depressive at best, and at worst, as schizophrenic. Consumers are much the same—they like consistency and predictability when they develop a relationship with a company or product. Establishing a friendship with customers is part of the brand goal. People can get very attached to brands, sharing much of their lives with them. Powerful bonds can be forged when brand and customer personalities merge.

Brand personality must be simple

A brand's personality must not be too complex. Although, human personality is extremely complex and hard to understand, it would be futile to try and project a brand personality that matches human complexity. The question often arises of how many personality characteristics a brand should have. There is no correct answer, but it is generally acknowledged that there should not be more than seven or eight characteristics, beyond which it becomes very difficult for the company to project the total personality without confusing the customer. It is better to focus on three or four personality characteristics and establish them well in people's minds than to try complicated communications activities aimed at projecting ten or more variables.

When a brand has too many characteristics, it will be difficult to live up to it as will be seen in a later discussion on the importance of "living" the brand personality. Limiting the number of personality characteristics does not necessarily restrict a brand's performance. The famous Marlboro brand stresses strength and independence—only two characteristics—but the branding has been managed so consistently well that it has been the world's second most valuable brand for many years.

Brand personality and brand values

When building brand identity, some companies choose brand values that are not personality characteristics. This is not uncommon in corporate brand building, especially if corporate values already exist. These values often flow naturally from the corporate vision or mission. For example, Hong Kong-based retailer and distributor Giordano, which has a vision of becoming the best and largest apparel company in the world, has core values of service, simplicity, speed, and value for money. Another example is Hong Kong Telecom, which has values of effectiveness, innovation, teamwork, customer focus, and integrity. There is nothing wrong with these non-personality values and they might even be the most expedient way to proceed. The values are imperative to operational efficiency and mission achievement, but such values may not produce a differentiated identity. Many companies have values such as commitment to excellence, quality, and service, since these are what many are striving for. So, non-personality values may be very worthwhile, however, they do not make a brand stand out from the crowd. In addition, these values refer primarily to the standards of operational performance that the company stands for, but not necessarily what the brand stands for. Hong Kong Telecom's mission is: "To deliver innovative communications services that enhance our customers' lifestyles and add value to their businesses." This is a very good mission statement, focusing entirely on the customer. But, corporate values can be enhanced by personality-based values that would relate more to, say, lifestyle aspirations.

Hence when building a brand, corporate values related to operational efficiency can be retained, but identity is better served by personality characteristics because these are very difficult to copy. It is most unlikely that a close competitor will have the same combination of personality characteristics, but it is highly likely that they have similar performance values and goals. Even if some of the personality characteristics happen to be the same, their execution is likely to be different. Personality is a priceless intangible asset that cannot be copied or owned by other companies. If created, nurtured, and managed well, it can generate lasting charisma for products and companies.

PERSONALITY, BRAND ASSOCIATIONS, AND SYMBOLIC MEANINGS

In Chapter 1, it was explained that the real essence of a brand is the values and associations that are wrapped around the basic product or service. The establishment of a brand personality brings these attachments to life by acting as symbols for the thoughts and fantasies of consumers who buy them.

Brand personality can strengthen the brand-customer relationship through the development of powerful emotional associations. These result from the pull of emotional appeal and can symbolize several things to people:

- what they stand for
- what they believe in
- what they care about
- what they love
- what they want to be
- the type of person they want to be with
- the kind of relationship they want
- what they want people to know about them
- the kind of friend they want

People yearn to possess famous brands for all these reasons and more. The following classification illustrates some of these inner needs and associations that people find brands express:

- loyal friend
- trusted partner
- heritage link
- cult of belonging
- feel-good factor
- dream team
- real me

The loyal friend

People sometimes feel lonely and need someone to talk to. Brands can become the kind of friend that fulfills this role. The brand a person always consumes can develop this relationship. It is a well-known fact that people talk to products such as cars, and about companies, as though they were friends. Research can elicit these thoughts by asking consumers to describe positive feelings about the brands they use, examples of replies being:

"I miss you when you're not with me."
"I have lots of fun with you."
"I can't wait until we see each other again."

Companies are also thought about in the same way.

It is worth asking what a conversation between a brand and a typical customer might be like. A company might find that the relationship is going through a bad patch, as one disappointed customer revealed when she said, "You were never there for me," referring to her bank.

Brands can be friends of not just individuals, but also of families. The Kellogg's Cornflakes packet on the breakfast table can be a welcome and reassuring sight, and some couples cannot actually converse until the Nescafé starts to take effect!

The trusted partner

As we grow up, we share our lives with others. Brands can fulfill a similar sharing role. Partnerships thrive on the feelings of appreciation and being valued by the other party. Brands often stimulate feelings of trust and reliability as customers walk in to a store, knowing that their brand will be there and that it will have the same outstanding quality when they use it. Companies that work hard on brand quality will reassure customers that they are valued, and the relationship will move from strength to strength.

The heritage link

The past is and will always be part of our lives, and people feel immense loyalty to their heritage. Some companies, for example

Harley Davidson, include patriotism as a brand personality characteristic. Others, such as American Athletics, include their country of origin in their name and communications. The power of heritage can be linked with the emotional pull of nostalgia. In some of Alfred Dunhill's advertisements are scenes of the beautiful English countryside and prestigious cars, emphasizing the scenes associated with the brand's home country. Pleasant memories move consumer minds. The new Volkswagen version of the legendary Beetle is all set to be a roaring success, bringing back fond memories of the 1960s and 1970s for many people. Brands like Mont Blanc and Parker combine fashion with nostalgia, when the older generation (grandparents or parents) used lovely writing instruments to write important documents.

The cult of belonging

Although every person is unique, each has the same need of wanting to be with others. We tend to have the need to belong or to associate ourselves with others, be it formally or informally. So we join clubs, get married, or become members of social or professional groups. Brands help satisfy this need by giving people the opportunity to join clans of their choice. Brand personalities provide the impetus for role modeling, and for becoming one of a special crowd. The Body Shop provides the opportunity to be active in saving the environment and protecting animals; Nike allows young people to be part of the sports club of their choice and be "friends" with their heroes; drink Pepsi and you are part of "Generation Next." When I was recently talking with the general manager of a listed Asian company, he referred to the brand of clothing he was wearing as "'my brand"—he was proud of belonging to the group of people who bought that particular brand. Brands provide instant membership of many fraternities.

The feel-good factor

Brands give everyone the chance to feel good in various ways and to express these positive feelings, thus reinforcing self-esteem. For example, someone might feel:

- sexy using Emporio Armani's 'he' or 'she' perfume
- rewarded, eating After Eight mints
- romantic, staying at Raffles Hotel
- youthful, taking a holiday at Club Med
- distinguished, driving a Jaguar
- successful, wearing a Rolex
- confident, drinking Johnny Walker Black Label
- trendy, buying a book from Amazon.com
- sporty, wearing Reebok trainers
- sophisticated, wearing Versace

The good thing about this is that the feelings brands evoke in people can become self-fulfilling. If you feel confident, you tend to act in a more confident manner. Brands can give people new capabilities and behaviors.

The dream team

Brands can take people to the dizzying heights of success that are the stuff of dreams. You can dress like the Hollywood stars, be part of the elite business community, and wear the same sports gear as the Olympians. Kids can become superstars just like their heroes. Nothing seems impossible when you buy the right brand. The use of real personalities, such as Michael Jordan, brings a brand to life and helps make dreams come true.

The real me

From aspiration to revelation, brands can reveal the real you. Brand choices reveal lifestyles, hopes, interests, and successes, and provide the opportunity for every person to express his or her own personality. The clothes you wear, the car you drive, the drinks you order, and the brands you buy paint a picture of the kind of person you are and the life you lead. Sometimes there is a difference between the "real me" as I normally am, and the "real me" I want to be. For example, at home I might just want to put on my favorite brand of jeans and T-shirt and relax—

because I feel that is the homely me—feeling comfortable with my friendly clothes and myself. For a dinner or cocktail party, I might wear a really smart, possibly stunning outfit because I want people to see the sophisticated part of me. Brands are the vehicles that allow everyone to show others what they are and can be like. Brands can help you say, "Hey, this is me!" in a variety of ways.

The holistic nature of brands

The aforementioned brand personalities are only stereotypes, but experience shows that they are typical of the impact that brands can have on everyone. It is not unusual for brands to evoke many such emotional associations in people, and to cause them psychologically or physically to act accordingly. While it is tempting to analyze brands by examining their individual aspects such as design, and logo, the strength of brands comes from the holistic way in which they attract and captivate consumers. The value of the brand to the individual who wants it is difficult to dissect and assess. It is this mysterious element that makes the world of brand building exciting and elusive. Despite this, companies are moving closer each year to assessing with greater precision which brand personalities will suit certain customer types.

Matching brand personality to customers

Customer profiling is a technique used by many world-class companies in building their brands. Market fragmentation, a global market trend identified in the introductory chapter, has made it imperative that companies understand the needs and wants of target customer groups. Companies involved in building and managing powerful brands are also skilled in matching the personality of their brands to that of the target customer groups. Matching both personalities increases the chances of success tremendously.

The precise identification of individual customer groups is called market segmentation, and this is discussed in detail in Chapter 3. Once defined, the job of the company then is to get to know as intimately as possible the members of the target segments. Harley Davidson did this by spending a substantial amount of time with bikers during weekends, accompanying them on trips, analyzing what they talked about, the plans they made, what they looked forward to doing, generally understanding every facet of their thinking. On the basis of that research, the personality characteristics of patriotic, free, male, macho, and heritage-oriented were born. This literally turned around and saved an ailing company.

BMW has also created different personalities for its different classes of cars based on the personalities of the separate market segments. This knowledge was gained by using psychographic segmentation methods, which will be explained in Chapter 3. Other companies are also going to extreme lengths to get inside the minds of consumers. Some are using opportunities to spend lengthy periods of time in people's homes, recording how they live and make their purchase decisions. These and other methods are discussed in the next chapter on understanding markets. But the procedure to follow in matching brands to customer personality is:

- define the target audience
- find out what they really need, want, and think
- build consumer profiles for each target audience
- create a relevant attractive brand personality
- project that personality appropriately and consistently

Some companies make it very clear in their advertising copy what their brand personality is, and to whom it should appeal. For example, part of a Maybelline print advertisement says:

Who is she?
She's a modern beauty.
She's smart, self-assured, and surprising.
…
Men are charmed by her.
Women admire her confidence."

Calvin Klein's Contradiction for Men states in its promotional material:

"He is modern with an edge
He combines strength with warmth
He is casual and sophisticated."

Both brands express their values to their target audience upfront. The values demonstrate clearly personality and aspirational positioning combinations that are potentially very powerful. Which woman or man would not choose to be like that? Maybelline's new print campaign is appearing in many Asian countries, and the copy is set alongside pictures of Hong Kong-based Eurasian model, Rosemary Vandenbrouke, the first time the New York-based cosmetics company has used an Asian face in its advertisements.

The bottom line is the brand experience

We have said that the quality of the brand has to be impressive relative to the competition. But, we have also argued that the brand experience is perhaps as much dependent, if not more, on the psychological as opposed to the physical. To the customer, a good brand experience can be more than just quality and function; it can be the:

- comments he or she gets from others
- admiring looks
- suggestive glances
- "me too" faces
- "wow" expressions
- secretive smiles
- jealous stares

They are all part of the rich fabric of the brand experience, appealing to the heart as well as the head, which determines the brand image. A strong sense of image can be developed in the minds of those who have not even experienced the product. However, the "perception of difference" created can be undone very quickly and negative reactions can be created if the eventual experience does not meet expectations.

CREATING THE BRAND EXPERIENCE

The branding experience is dependent on the continuing satisfaction of the customer's needs. These needs include the functional needs associated with buying the product or service, and the emotional needs and associations derived from the brand. If the product is the subject of the brand, the main factors are quality, availability, and reinforcement of the brand values and personality through consistent and appropriate advertising and promotion. If the brand is a service, then service quality standards replace those of product quality. In Chapter 7, the case study of lifestyle and fashion clothing brand Nautica addresses the prerequisites for the creation of a successful international brand.

However, it must be stressed here that for corporate brand image to occupy consistently high ratings, especially in services, the employees of the company must "live" the brand values and personality. This has to be followed up with a brand culture which involves applying the brand values to every aspect of organizational life. This important topic is covered in Chapter 5 on Brand Management.

Branding technology companies and products

Branding is traditionally linked with fast-moving consumer products, but nowadays technology forms an expanding component of many consumer products. The proliferation of technological advances and the speed of technological change have led to the shortening of product life cycles, resulting in technology products behaving more like traditional consumer goods. The branding of technology products like computers, however, has more problems to be overcome in the minds of the ordinary person than that associated with the usual consumer products, like packaged foods and healthcare products. The main problem that needs to be overcome is people's fear of technology. As people do not understand it, they do not trust it. The fear can originate from two sources. First, when buying a technology product, the customer is worried whether it will actually perform properly. Second, the fear arises from a lack of brand identity—not really knowing the brand. This is seemingly bad news to brand builders, who rely on generating trust in the product- or company-customer relationship.

Another problem for technology brand builders is that branding has traditionally always been successful when executed in a consistent manner. Consistency is the golden rule of branding. Technology, on the other hand, owes its success to change rather than consistency. The dilemma faced when branding technology products is how to reconcile consistency with change in the branding process. In the high-powered sales pitch for the latest computer model, the vague knowledge of impending obsolescence is a consumer concern that is rarely addressed. With a product life cycle of only six months and a constant leap-frogging of technology advances, maintaining brand loyalty is a real problem. This confusion among consumers is compounded when customers realize that many of the leading brands outsource a large proportion, if not all, of their production.

Finally, there is a difference in the buying behavior of consumers when they buy ordinary consumer product as opposed to technology products. Consumer-product buying behavior is often impulsive, whereas purchase decisions for technology products are more carefully considered. This deliberation increases as the technology products move from the domain of personal to business use.

The remedy to the problems faced when branding technology products is that technology companies must build a strong brand image and excellent customer relationships. In addition, companies must address the usage and psychological aspects of fear, which are so important in the brand-choice decision. Presently, there is plenty of room for developing a competitive advantage based on service capability and speed of response to customer problems. This is especially true for computer products.

In a later chapter the execution of brand strategy will be discussed. Yet another remedy is to bring emotion into the customer experience. This can involve creating a likable personality for the company that will be inherited by its products, which is what Nokia is trying to do with its concentration on "human technology." Sony Corporation has managed to meet the challenge by concentrating on the quality image of its products, as has Intel. Compaq is driving hard on service quality. According to these approaches to branding, quality assurance seems to be the major concern of technology consumers. Sony and Intel have also worked hard on their other brand values and now stand among the top-ranked brands in the world.

QUESTIONS CONSUMERS MIGHT ASK THEMSELVES ABOUT A BRAND

Companies should think about the people who buy or may be persuaded to buy their brand, because these customers will be thinking about the company. Here are some of the thoughts and questions that may pass through customers' minds, consciously or subconsciously. The more a company understands the customer's thought process, the more successful it will be in branding.

- What do the brand and I have in common?
- What will the brand do for me?
- What will the brand say about me?
- What part of my life does the brand fit in to?
- Will the brand help me become someone I want to be?
- Does the brand fit my personality?
- Can I rely on this brand?
- Is the brand available wherever I go?
- Is the brand my friend?
- Will my friends like the brand?
- Does the brand make me stand out from the crowd?
- Does the brand make me part of a community?
- Will the brand bring me recognition?

QUESTIONS A COMPANY SHOULD ASK ABOUT ITS BRAND

- What is your brand vision?
- How does it relate to your corporate vision?
- What needs and wants of consumers will the brand satisfy?
- What are the brand's rational and emotional aspects (the *yin* and *yang*)?

- Can you define the essential personality or identity of your brand?
- What makes your brand better than competing brands?
- What makes your brand different from competing brands?
- What will you never change about your brand?
- Why do some people prefer other brands to yours?

In the case of Singapore's National Computer Systems, the corporate brand-building process was made more difficult by the fact that the company had to re-position itself and change its image and market perception. Analyzing how it achieved this will help many Asian companies facing similar problems. Expressions International is the second case study, and it shows how a successful brand has been built around a distinctive personality.

Case Study 1

NATIONAL COMPUTER SYSTEMS
Building a brand and changing market
perceptions after corporatization

National Computer Systems (NCS) is a Singapore company that has gone through more change than most over the last few years, having been the subject of a privatization exercise in 1996 when it was split from the National Computer Board (NCB). Now a part of the huge Singapore Telecom group, NCS has had to battle against the odds to become a regional market leader and achieve commercial success.

Identity crisis

Branding became an important fundamental issue, as NCS quickly realized that this entailed more than visual identity changes and new communications collateral. The main obstacles that had to be overcome were:

- the mindset of the employees
- the perceptions held by customers in the market place

The two were related and a source of mutual reinforcement. Changing the mindset of the staff meant getting them to move beyond the world of government and into developing a more commercial outlook. This has proven to be an ongoing process, which would have been more difficult had the age profile of the staff not been fairly low. Recruitment of staff from outside the company as it grew has helped to inject fresh thinking, as has a comprehensive change-management program.

A shift in corporate image was more difficult to accomplish, as entrenched perceptions are not easily changed. While it was part of NCB, NCS carried out systems integration work for the government of Singapore, known around the world as being an advanced high-technology country. This work placed NCS as a world leader in terms of public-sector IT development, as it was responsible for the biggest computerization project in Singapore—the Civil Service Computerization Program.

But this success was a double-edged sword—proving an exceptional accomplishment on the one hand, and yet invoking a perception that here was a former government organization now trying to make money out of the private sector. Staff who had to market NCS's services came up against these negative associations commercially. So, NCS had the difficult task of trying to establish its own brand name and reputation, and distancing itself from its heritage, while at the same time relying on the heritage for track record purposes. This situation was made more difficult when NCS was bought over by Singapore Telecom, and it belonged to another form of monopoly.

Branding intangible services

Another problem NCS discovered was the difficulty in branding a company that marketed intangible services as opposed to one that delivered tangible products. While not producing anything of its own, NCS sources world-class technology to deliver innovative solutions to client problems. So, what do you do to differentiate a company from others when all it can do is sell solutions, which other players are also doing? NCS decided that building the personality of the brand was to be the key agent in establishing a strong differentiated image. Early advertising focused on this, with the projection of personality characteristics such as:

• innovative
• successful
• energetic
• professional
• full of drive
• dependable

NCS's advertising campaign used shots of actual staff. Public relations also played an important part in managing perceptions. This was done by:

• building a relationship with the media
• holding seminars and customer forums
• giving talks
• writing articles in various publications
• participating in exhibitions
• visiting companies to develop corporate relationships

All these activities had been carefully designed to support the brand proposition of turning IT into innovations, and creating business value for customers. There is still some way to go towards developing the brand personality. However, brand awareness has risen considerably, and the market place is not questioning NCS's parentage as much as before.

NCS is now accepted as a good service provider. It has tried hard to get customers to see it as a partner that helps bring their business plans to fruition. Customers feel they now have more choice than before. Past NCS customers have come to terms with the changes, and new customers perceive the company to be a major IT-services provider. So, NCS has been on a long and winding road to prove its commercial worth and manage the perceptions of its different target audiences. As it is a continuing process, the company knows there are still many things it has to do. Developing a customer-service orientation is its new priority, and as Chief Executive Officer KC Lee says: "We must continually raise the bar, and become more aggressive in looking after our customers."

Reaching out—Filling the gap in the Asian market

NCS is also making rapid progress outside Singapore. The regional association of Singapore with technology adds a positive dimension to the past history of NCS. And the clear ability of NCS to understand the needs of Asian companies is proving to be a strategic competitive advantage. It has the experience of dealing with complex and sensitive government-related sectors such as healthcare and immigration, and with private sector problems, too. It can leverage the world-class products it has access to and build solutions to suit local needs. Perceptions are, therefore, different, with NCS being seen as young, positive, reliable, intelligent, understanding, and from good parentage.

NCS has positioned itself as an expert manager of large-scale, complex projects on the basis of its track record, and has a solid reputation for reliability, an attribute that is vital for any IT-based company. The "Made in Singapore" label is a definite plus, and as there are at present few reliable IT service providers, NCS is successfully exploiting a gap in the market.

As to long-term ambitions, NCS wants to be a global player, but first has the immediate goal of placing itself in the top five in the Asia Pacific region. And NCS is getting there.

Brand strengths: long-term brand investment, persistence, attention to brand culture, good use of public relations in brand building.

Case Study 2

EXPRESSIONS INTERNATIONAL
Branding and positioning
lifestyle products and services

After the delivery of her second child in 1989 Theresa Chew suffered health problems. The problems were severe enough for her to search the world for cures to her ailments. She found one in the U.S., and her new business life was born. Already a businesswoman, she decided to venture into the wellness business and has never looked back. Now she helps others take charge of their lives through her lifestyle business, Expressions International, and its associated product ranges. Although not formally trained in marketing techniques, Theresa has, nevertheless, been successful in establishing a strong brand. And in recent years, the company has expanded from providing wellness and weight-management facilities to offering facial salons and spas. Like any successful entrepreneur, Theresa has a passion for her business, which drives and motivates not just her and her employees, but anyone who meets her.

All brands have to perform, and the Expressions experience works, as many testimonials and success stories have proved. Nevertheless, there is a great deal of competition in the health, beauty, and fitness (wellness) industry. Differentiation was an essential part of the company's progress. The product benefits of looking and feeling good, and even the term "wellness" are used by others. Branding the business was the key to differentiation. As with most businesses, the "hardware" in terms of equipment, facilities, and product quality can easily be matched by competitors. But the "software" of emotional associations and feelings towards the brand is more difficult to replicate.

Isolating and then building the brand values were critical. The chosen brand values are a mixture of existing ones, and some that would enhance the customer experience and position the business away from the competition. Expressions International's brand values are:

- premiumship
- professionalism
- innovativeness
- knowledge
- leadership
- natural
- holistic
- renewal
- inspirational
- empathy
- new age wellness

As can be seen, the brand values are numerous and are a mixture of corporate and personality values and characteristics. The large number of values makes it more difficult to express all of them in the brand experience. However, having established them, Expressions turned its attention to applying these values to every aspect of the business, including:

- the interior and ambience of its studios and offices
- any objects and ornaments
- color schemes
- relationship of staff with customers, and staff product knowledge, attitude.

- language used in the media
- staff clothing and presentation
- music
- senses
- location and look of premises

As all of these aspects have an impact on the customer experience, each had to be scrutinized and adjusted accordingly. The results have definitely given Expressions the competitive edge, and paved the way for further expansion.

Managing the brand has now become more important. Because of the need for consistency in brand personality, positioning, and consumer experience, the company has expanded from franchising to brand licensing, where it can totally control the brand image, while still giving investment partners the returns they expect.

Already a regional player, Expressions' founder and CEO, Theresa Chew is an ambitious person, thinking "brand" all the time. Thus, it would not be surprising to see the company become a truly international lifestyle brand.

Brand strengths: CEO passion, differentiation from competitors, brand analysis and implementation.

3

Understanding Markets

THE IMPORTANCE OF SEGMENTATION IN BRANDING

An essential technique for successful branding is market segmentation. This chapter is titled Understanding Markets because this is precisely how market segmentation assists companies. It has already been emphasized that market fragmentation is increasing while homogenous mass markets are becoming increasingly rare. Gone are the days when everyone used the same toothpaste or shampoo. Consumers the world over, while gravitating towards globally similar products, are increasingly wanting these to be tailored to suit their various preferences and tastes. Market segmentation has now become the norm. Segmentation is a customer-driven approach towards marketing. It is different from having a variety of products on offer—a product-driven approach—without knowing what people really want. Segmentation is about market differentiation, not product differentiation.

Without some form of market segmentation, companies can end up with a product-driven rather than customer-driven organization, resulting in

- a fuzzy or even poor image
- falling sales
- disappointing market share
- excessive customer complaints

- declining profitability
- brand failure

Segmentation is the process where markets are analyzed and divided into groups of potential or actual customers with similar characteristics, needs and wants, and who—because of these differences—act differently when purchasing products and services. When executed well, segmentation helps companies to predict these different behaviors with greater accuracy.

Benefits of market segmentation

Helps select target markets

Segmentation is sometimes referred to as selective marketing because it aids the selection of target markets. Companies cannot target every customer as explained above, but with segmentation studies, they can select the most attractive parts of a total market. The attraction can be based on the following.

- Growth: Companies can select segments that are growing faster than the general market. One feature of modern market dynamics is that some customer groups or segments are fast growing while others are stable or even in decline. For example, a few years ago, China had no yuppie class (young, urban professionals, with high disposable incomes, on their way up the corporate ladder), but now there are close to 100 million yuppies. Companies need to be aware of growth patterns in the various segments and the new segments that are emerging.
- Profitability: By observing segment purchasing patterns, companies can concentrate on the segments that generate greater purchases. This is the volume approach, which leads to cost reductions. Companies may also find certain segments that are willing to pay premium prices. For the special attention they receive, consumers in niche-market segments are often prepared to pay premium prices. This, too, can increase profitability.

- Brand fit: Companies can choose the segments that most closely resemble their brand identity or personality. Much of brand success is achieved by appealing to the emotional and psychological aspects of the human mind and matching brand personality with that of the consumer; segmentation brings brands and people closer together and with greater accuracy.

Gives company focus

This is the laser-missile approach, as opposed to the blanket-bomb approach. When the target market is narrowed down, it becomes easier to attack with specific objectives and plans. It also becomes easier to tailor product offerings and distribution channels. For instance, Citibank in Malaysia has only three branches, and yet has the leading market share of the housing-loan segments it target. Citibank understands its customers wants, and markets its product through cost-effective direct marketing. As a consequence of the tremendous focus that segmentation brings, it also becomes easier to measure performance vis-à-vis competitors.

Helps small companies find niche-markets

Segmentation helps smaller companies find niche-markets. There is little difference, if any, between segmentation and niche marketing. Niche marketing is an essential strategy for small- and medium-sized businesses, and segmentation is the best way to find niche-markets. Once found, niche-markets are easier to defend against powerful competitors. This is partly due to the fact that niche-markets often exist because people's needs and wants have not been fully satisfied. If a company can serve a particular segment well, it has a greater chance of establishing and maintaining brand loyalty.

Facilitates efficient and effective brand positioning

Segmentation facilitates more efficient and effective brand positioning. By understanding a specific market segment well, information such as lifestyle data can increase the effectiveness of advertising and promotion, thus, avoiding waste of money and other resources. Such understanding helps insure that the right messages get to the right people via the right medium.

Aids marketing to several groups

For brand development purposes, market segmentation allows companies to market their brands to more than one customer group, depending on their unique needs and wants. This market differentiation can provide the rationale for line and brand extensions, and subsequent phenomenal business growth.

It is particularly important for Asian companies to find suitable market segments for their regional and international expansion so that they avoid head-on clashes with giant global brands which are aiming for universal segments or have a stranglehold on certain types of customer. It is equally important for the already established international brand to seek new opportunities.

SEGMENTATION PREREQUISITES

Before moving on to the discussion of the various methods of segmenting markets, it is worth remembering that certain fundamentals are required for segmentation to be successful.

- First, each segment or group of people must exhibit different behavior. This may or may not be easy to measure. For instance, age group is an easier measure than lifestyle factors.

- Second, each segment has to be of sufficient size to make it worth targeting. Kellogg's, for example, would look at population size before deciding to enter a market.

- Third, the life of the segment must be long enough to provide a suitable return on the investment incurred for penetration and maintenance of a good market share. Although needs and wants evolve over time, a certain degree of stability is highly desirable. If competition is already intense, it might not be worth the effort and resources needed to access the market and acquire the necessary volume. There must also be the prospect of further growth in the segment to make it worthwhile.

- Lastly, accessibility is essential for communications purposes. In some countries, media availability is restricted or underdeveloped. For example, it is difficult to advertise women's personal hygiene products in some Muslim countries.

SEGMENTATION, MARKETING PLANNING, AND BRAND PORTFOLIOS

Because of the popularity of segmentation, it has become an integral part of marketing planning. Segmentation can provide valuable data for strategic decision-making and brand resource allocation as the following example shows. Assume that a company operates in one market or market category. The company has discovered that this market has been growing steadily at 8% each year and is forecast to do so for the next three years. A recent segmentation study reveals three distinct customer groups of similar size. The growth rates of the three segments are measured and it is found that segment A has been growing at the market rate of 8% while segments B and C grew at 6% and 10% respectively. Had the company known this much earlier, it could have directed more of its marketing effort at segment C to give it a higher overall market share.

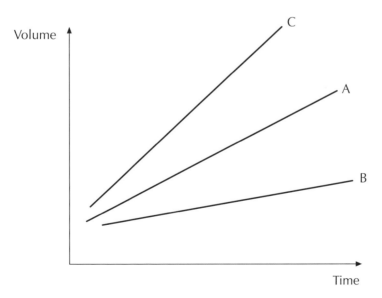

Figure 5: Market segment growth rates.

The situation could have been worse had all of the company's customers belonged to segment B and the company not measured the rate of growth of the total market. The result would then have seen the company commanding a decreasing share of an increasing market. In absolute terms, the company's sales volume would have risen steadily, leading it to think that it was doing well, which in turn could have led to complacency when, in fact, its competitors were doing very much better. Both scenarios have been known to happen. The point is that within a given market there are segments that grow at different rates, and companies must be alert by keeping track of such data.

In reality, companies often have more than one brand in their portfolio, and therefore, need to keep a close watch of more than one market. In many fast-moving consumer goods markets, such as the breakfast-cereals market, companies often try to increase overall market share by having more than one brand in the same market or category. These complementary brands are deliberately positioned to attract different market segments so that they do not cannibalize each other's sales, but instead attack competitors in each segment.

MARKET SEGMENTATION METHODS

There are many ways in which market segmentation can be accomplished—from a broad-brush approach down to reaching the segment of one. Some of these methods require relatively simple research procedures while others require more complex methodologies. A discussion of the most commonly used approaches follows.

Demographic segmentation

This method can include a whole host of variables such as market size, age, gender, marital status, income level, and occupation, either on their own or in combination with each other. It is amazing how some companies turn potentially unattractive segments into opportunities. Kodak in India found that few of the 950 million Indians could afford a camera, a fact that at first posed a headache for the company's camera sales growth plans in India. But, Kodak came upon a solution, now on trial, involving the rental of cameras. This is proving to be so successful that it is now being tested in Russia and South America.

Age segmentation is another popular method. Both small- and big-brand companies pursue children, in particular, with great vigor. This is hardly surprising looking at the statistics. In the U.S. alone in 1997, parents spent more than US$500 billion on items purchased upon the prompting of their children (under 12 years of age). This figure is expected to rise to US$1 trillion by 2002. Research shows that some children start developing an association with a particular brand by the age of two years, and face peer pressure from the age of three. By 2010, there will be 30 million teenagers in the U.S.. Coca-Cola, Levi Strauss, Microsoft, Guess, Gap, and many other companies research and target various age groups for these lucrative reasons. Most soft drinks (except diet varieties) are targeted at 12–24-year-olds, and MTV aims for the 15–34-year-olds. Teen magazines are enjoying unprecedented growth levels, and Barbie dolls sell more every year. Roughly half of the Southeast Asian population is under 25 years of age, and two-third under 35 years. Spirits and liquor manufacturers, including that of Pernod, are targeting 18–25-year-olds because this is the age when drinking habits and liquor-repertoire form. It is based on these habits and repertoire, which will follow them throughout their lives, that future choices are made, depending on mood and occasion.

Another major factor in age segmentation is longer life expectancy. In Japan, the fastest-growing market segment is the over 70-year-olds. Countries targeting Japanese tourists are now paying special attention to this "gray" customer group. In other countries the older age groups are also growing fast. In the U.S. by 2005, the number of people reaching the age of 50 (baby-boomers) will be 42% of the adult population, up from the current level of about 37%. Seeing this burgeoning market segment, even alcoholic-beverage producers such as Anheuser-Busch are targeting the group with a new light beer called Catalina Blonde. Age-segmentation research is a big and growing business.

Gender has always been another segment separator. Many brands such as Nike, Armani, and Tommy Hilfiger have extended their product range to cater to women. The female market is becoming very important in the U.S., where 80% of all consumer spending and 75% of healthcare spending is decided by women. This is causing a profound impact on the way in which brands communicate with their target audiences. Within a gender-related segment, it is possible to have sub-segments. For example, stationery maker Sanrio Co of Japan has a core segment of children to which it markets the cartoon, Hello Kitty. It has recently successfully moved into the segments of teenagers and women in their 20s, with plans to provide more products for adults. Sanrio also intends to increase the number of its stores that target women. (See the case study at the end of this chapter.)

Demographic segmentation can be very useful, and its effectiveness can often be enhanced by combining it with other methods. *FHM* magazine, for instance is targeted at males, mainly below the age of 30 and with an average monthly income of RM2,500 and above. It is an international brand published in the U.K., France, Germany, Australia, Singapore, and Malaysia. It also combines lifestyle and personality segmentation, providing features that are practical, sexy, and funny to a typical reader who is intelligent, has a zest for life, and a healthy sense of humor. Based on this sub-segment, *FHM* offers features on music, movies, fashion, health, true stories, jokes, thrills, sports, computers, and finance. In another example, Panasonic in the U.S. is buying advertisements on news and sports shows watched by men in households with annual incomes exceeding US$55,000.

Geographic segmentation

This type of segmentation concentrates on dividing markets into geographic regions such as cities, urban and rural locations, countries, etc. It is often used in combination with other methods to determine, for instance, the number of rural people with various income levels. This method is popular due to the cheap and easily available information. In the developing countries of Asia, there is a trend towards growing urbanization, with more young people leaving their hometowns in the countryside to seek work in major cities.

In Asia, there appears to be two segments that are large and of interest to many companies. One consists of high-net-worth individuals who have been educated abroad and are well traveled. They tend to have acquired their wealth through inheritance or taking over family businesses, or they can be the *nouveau riche* who have suddenly acquired wealth as a result of several years of the Asian business boom. Some of them have been hit by the recession of the late 1990s, but most have survived with their wealth intact even if their businesses have suffered. This broad segment shares similar international preferences, attitudes, and interests with other similar segments around the world. They usually buy luxury brands, usually of western origin.

The second segment is the youth group—teenagers who tend to be well educated and identify with their Western counterparts, although their behavior may be partly influenced by family, as seen in Levi's case study at the end of this chapter. Even in Japan, which in the past has been noted for its conformity, there now exists a segment of rebellious youth called *shinjinrui*.

Geodemographic segmentation

The basis of this segmentation is the division of the population into residential areas. PRIZM of the U.S. and ACORN of U.K. are two well-known providers of geodemographic segmentation information. This information can be useful in isolating very specific customer groups, for example, in determining the number of single females living with relatives, having an income of less than $X, and residing within two miles of the city centre. This segmentation method can be useful for direct marketing and decisions such as establishing a new retail or professional practice outlet.

Corporate segmentation

Businesses can also be segmented for branding purposes. In this case, information is gathered on variables such as:

* size—in terms of revenue, profit, net worth
* growth rates—same, fast, slow, static
* geographical—domestic, national, regional, international, global
* industry type—manufacturing, microelectronics, plastics, financial services
* ownership—sole, partnership, family, listed

- age and behavior of management—young, aggressive, cautious, risk-taking, innovative, traditional, older, clannish, community service-oriented or cause-oriented.

There are, no doubt, many other variables that could be added to this list. The point about segmenting markets, whatever the line of business, is it pays to have as much information on the customer as possible.

Socio-cultural segmentation

Markets are segregated by factors such as social class, racial group, religion, and culture. Many companies are now finding this method of segmentation useful, and some are calling it "minority marketing." In the U.S, a lot of attention is being given to the differing needs of African-Americans, Asian Americans, and Hispanic Americans. There are even sub-segments within these groups. Within the Hispanic segment, for instance, there are Mexican, Cuban, and Puerto Rican sub-segments. Companies that concentrate on building an international brand will have to pay special attention to these socio-cultural factors and others, as they will almost certainly vary from country to country. For example, some countries value individualism, while others value collectivism. In India, for example, McDonald's burgers are made from mutton, instead beef or pork, so as not to offend prevalent religious principles. Other examples of how international brands adapt to local socio-cultural circumstances are scattered throughout this book.

Price-sensitivity segmentation

Consumers can also be segmented by price. This is often linked to the benefits offered. Airlines practice this kind of segmentation with First, Business, Economy, and in some cases, Super Economy classes. Some airlines also have differential pricing for advance bookings as against standby ticketing. For example, British Airways has created sub-brands of First, Club Class, and World Traveler for long-haul routes. Customers buying each of the brands get various privileges for the differential brand pricing, and the brands have totally separate brand management.

Benefits segmentation

In benefits segmentation, markets are segmented by the benefits expected by consumers. Benefits segmentation is based on the consumers' question: "What's in it for me?". Benefits are advantages that consumers expect to derive from the product or company experience. Sometimes consumers do not really want the product or service, but are attracted by the benefits they will receive from purchasing the product or service. They might not want a life insurance policy, but they do want peace of mind. They might not like using ATMs, but they see the benefit of convenience. Benefits segmentation can be used for a range of purposes, and its aim is to find out the purpose behind consumer behavior. It can also be used for business-to-business marketing, to establish the importance of services such as technical and service support, and to test the acceptability of new products and services, for example, the leasing computer equipment to certain clients.

One of the drawbacks of benefits segmentation is the occasional difficulty in establishing the real reason behind the purchase decision, as people may say one thing and do another. It is, therefore, wise to try and establish desire as well as purpose. For example, people might agree that buying a life insurance policy is a wise investment, but this may not be enough to persuade them to buy it. However, when presented with the scenario of trying to survive without an income, the family might be more persuaded by the benefit of having peace of mind. Benefit segmentation must, therefore, aim to establish the emotional as well as the rational benefits that are relevant and appeal to each target audience.

A benefit of some luxury purchases is its investment value. New limited-edition pens like Mont Blanc's 75th Anniversary collection, are expected to increase rapidly in value with time, and in Singapore it was sold out before it was even displayed at the shops.

User-behavior segmentation

Companies can obtain useful segmentation data by analyzing why and when people buy products and services, and even the occasions of usage. Who uses your product or service? Are they light, medium, or heavy users? How much loyalty do they have towards your brand? What is the ratio of usage of your brand compared to the competition? Does usage vary with location? Or by application? An example of the latter is the consumption of soups as snacks, small meals, starters, and post-operation nourishment. Behavioral segmentation is adaptable and relatively low cost—point-of-sale data gathering is now very sophisticated—but the right question needs to be asked. Using the example of pens, people buy different styles for different occasions—social events, for ordinary work, important business occasions.

Family-life-cycle segmentation

This segmentation approach is based on human progression through family life and the various stages that influence buying behavior. It is an interesting approach—demographics with an interesting twist. It has been used successfully by financial services companies, and is useful for other industries also. The basic framework is as follows.

- Singles—this group does not have large financial debts, likes lifestyle and fashion products, and can be opinion leaders and early adopters of new trends.
- Newly married couples, with no children—they usually have double incomes, are interested in consumer durables such as cars and home-building items, tend to have frequent holidays, and will buy houses.
- Full nest one—this group consists of married couples with their youngest child under the age of six. Home purchase is a priority, and cash is often short as one partner often gives up work. This group buys household necessities and child-related products.
- Full nest two—the youngest child in this group of married couples with children is over the age of six. The family is usually financially better off as both parents work. Education and home items are priorities.
- Full nest three—this group consists of older couples with older but still dependent children. Financially, this group is usually better off, and purchase consumer durables, such as second cars and furniture. Education is a priority.

- Empty nest one—in this group, the children have left home, and savings, therefore, increase. Buying another home is considered, and the group tends to purchase the things it has missed like vacations and luxury goods.

- Empty nest two—the main breadwinner has retired, so financial resources are scarce. Medical and other health-related products are frequent purchases.

- Solitary survivor (working)—he or she can manage financially, but often homes are sold.

- Solitary survivor (retired)—income reduction forces only necessary purchases and medical aid.

This approach like all other segmentation methods, is generalized and there may be exceptions that do not fit in to the categories. Despite this, it can be a useful tool for predicting the type of products and services people will want at certain stages of their lives.

Psychographic segmentation

Psychographics is the most exciting development in the segmentation technique for brand building. It is especially relevant to Asian companies that seek to develop international brands, and to international companies that wish to establish a growing brand presence in Asia. Psychographics covers many factors including activities, interests, opinions, attitudes, values, and lifestyles. The beauty of it lies in the combination of personality data with motivational and behavioral activity. Psychographics helps in the understanding of why people behave the way they do, and therefore, in understanding the markets, which are made of people. The advantages of psychographic segmentation are:

- it can find new markets, whereas other methods such as demographics deal with existing markets

- as it uncovers consumer thinking and motivations that govern consumer dynamics, it, therefore, can explain why various markets exist

- it explains consumer behavior, including perceptions, needs, motivations, preferences, brand awareness, and loyalty
- it greatly assists in the creation of accurate positioning strategies, leading to focused and effective communications
- it can facilitate brand-personality creation and development
- it can help position new brands and re-position old ones
- it can reveal strategic positioning opportunities
- it can discover better ways of brand distribution

Psychographics is not, however, a panacea for niche marketing, branding, and positioning. There are many approaches and no one ideal way of going about it. The data gathered is usually not universally applicable, as lifestyles, attitudes, and other elements can differ from region to region and even from town to town. So, while psychographics offers a much greater understanding of the human mind and consumers' brand-related behavior, its predictive qualities are somewhat generalized. The remaining disadvantage is the cost of psychographic surveys, which can be on the high side as they tend to involve large question inventories that have to be tailored to specific brand issues. However, this has to be weighed against the fact that new brand launches and campaigns to strengthen existing brands are likely to be more successful when the maximum information is known about the nuances in consumer thinking.

Psychographics need not be complicated, however. Attitudes, interests, and lifestyles are aspects of this methodology that can sometimes be easily identified without a great deal of survey work. For example, there is a growing business in eco-tourism purely because of changing attitudes towards the environment and how people value it. This segment covers all age groups, from teenagers to those over 60 years old, although it is very popular with the 19–35-year age group. Asia is a natural venue for this kind of tourism, offering many destinations and alternative activities. This growing segment of the industry is named "The Adventure Traveler" by experts like the magazine *Blue*, which caters solely to this niche. People in this segment might cycle through China, surf in Bali, trek in the Indonesian jungles, climb mountains in

India, scuba dive in the Maldives, or visit many other destinations and activities.

Before looking at psychographic methods in greater detail, we should mention lifestyle segmentation. Some experts say that lifestyle analysis is a part of psychographics, while others believe it should be treated separately. I believe the way people live their lives (or want to live their lives) influences their brand-purchase decision-making in the same way that their attitudes, interests, and opinions do. As psychographics concerns the causes of behavior, lifestyle should then be included in the same category. For example, the health-conscious segment of the population desire healthy lifestyles and this drives their behavior, not just in terms of which activities they get involved in, but also what brands they buy. Lifestyle brands can bring huge monetary rewards. TAG Heuer has been associated with sporting excellence since 1860, and promotes its watches using famous sports personalities. It sells some 700,000 watches a year. The agreement by Polo Ralph Lauren to buy the Club Monaco brand—which makes and markets clothing, cosmetics, and home furnishings—was said by Chairman and Chief Executive Ralph Lauren to be a tremendous growth opportunity to build another lifestyle brand.

Values and lifestyles

Syndicated research studies, which are not as costly as individually commissioned studies because many companies contribute to the syndicated ones, e.g. VALS2 (values and lifestyles) by Stanford Research Institute, produce a classification based on attitude, behavior, and how people make decisions. It is a detailed categorization explained only briefly here. It includes the following segments:

- actualizers—independent people, who tend to exercise leadership and are risk-takers
- fulfilleds—very organized and self-assured people who tend to be intellectual
- believers—people who are the respectful and loyal types
- achievers—people who are practical and follow convention, but are very brand conscious

- strivers—sociable people with aspirations and who follow trends
- experiencers—impulsive people who tend to be impatient
- makers—people who are mainly concerned with family and are practical and self-sufficient
- strugglers—very cautious and conservative people who tend to conform and be one of the crowd

Other well-known values and lifestyle studies include the Yankelovich Monitor, which surveys consumer marketing-related social trends, and LOV (The List of Values) developed at the University of Michigan. There are many more classifications that have been developed for specific markets.

Lifestyle changes

There is a growing interest in lifestyle change marketing, which sometimes appears under the title of synchrographics. This area of research is slightly similar to the family-life-cycle studies, and may overlap to a certain extent. However, synchrographics looks more at the dynamics of personal change—personal lives as opposed to family lives—that promote changes in lifestyle behavior, and hence, buying behavior. For example, events that might trigger lifestyle changes at particular times, such as at the beginning of university life, getting the first job, being laid off, getting married or divorced, having children, retiring, moving to another country, or the death of a close relative affect mental states, buying power, and the nature of items bought.

Asian applicability

Many of the psychographic studies of values and lifestyles like VALS2 are applied around the world, even though the values are typical in a statistical sense only of the U.S. population. Despite this, classifications are helpful to Asian companies because they tend to be universally valid when applied to strategic positioning and new product development. However it should be noted that such psychographic research-based segmentation, while proven to be very valuable for the reasons given above, can differ among countries, so country-by-country research is advisable. Communicating psychographic brand values through advertising, for example, cannot be done in a uniform way, as cultural differences and acceptance can vary enormously. There are many cultural and significant behavioral differences even between neighboring countries such as Singapore and Malaysia, for example, let alone diverse ones across the world.

In particular, some areas to watch out for in international application are typified in the following instances:

- translation problems—for example, achievement, although a universal value, translates into inner harmony and personal attainment in Japan
- romance and sex—underplayed in China, but acceptable in Japan
- individualism versus collectivism—the value of belonging is universal, but doing your own thing is usually frowned upon in Asia, where the family and groupings take precedence over the individual
- feelings—personal happiness is a life goal for the individual in the West, but superceded by obligations in the East.

As values, attitudes, interests, opinions, and lifestyles change with time, frequent research is recommended. Asian companies wishing to become global or international players would be wise to invest in macro- and micro-research in each country they wish to enter. The results, from my experience, justify the investment.

Other approaches to psychographic segmentation follow.

Brand-personality-relationship segmentation

People develop relationships with brands—this is the real purpose of branding. It is, therefore, possible for companies to segment their customer bases by the way in which consumers perceive that relationship. On a very simplistic level, this could be statements of consumers' likes or dislikes of the brand. But, psychographic research often goes deeper than that in order to understand the reasons why people feel and behave as they do. If a brand is perceived as being warm and friendly, the company would want to know why so that its marketing communications can reinforce that relationship. A company would also like to make sure that it does not undertake any action that might destroy the relationship positioning its brand has in consumers' minds, such as changing the packaging to a cold color or adding more technology into customer interactions with the company. Perceptual mapping, which is described with examples in Chapter 6, is one of the techniques that can give clear indications of how different people view the various brands and personality relationships.

Personality and attitudinal characteristics

Many studies have been developed to segment people by personality characteristics: extrovert, introvert, ambitious, adventurous, and others. Companies use this segmentation for many purposes including recruitment. Attitudes towards buying new products is interesting, with people demonstrating different inclinations which can be classified as:

- innovators
- early adopters
- early majority
- late majority
- laggards

Attitudes towards the purchase of specific products can also be analyzed, as Dell Computer did when it found personality types with attitudes such as wanting

- ease of use
- any computer that will work
- compatible hardware and software as needed by network technicians
- the best quality available for particular purposes
- the latest features and gadgets

To briefly summarize psychographics, it is essentially generalized because every person is different. As most studies include present behavior, personality types, and aspirations, psychographics is becoming increasingly important as a predictive, rather than descriptive tool. It is also valid worldwide and can be used for international segmentation studies, with allowances for cultural differences.

Most research agencies and large advertising agencies tend to have their own instruments, and it is worth while looking at a selection of them if you seriously wish to research a market in this way.

SOME BASIC QUESTIONS ON UNDERSTANDING MARKETS

- Which markets do we want to access?
- Have we got enough macro- and micro-data to make segmentation decisions on these markets and choose our priorities?
- How can we divide these markets for our products or services into groups of customers whose needs might differ?
- How can we modify our products/services to make them more attractive to each separate group? By changing
  - performance levels?
  - design?
  - support?
  - speed of service?
  - packaging?
  - positioning?
  - the price we charge in each segment? Is there an opportunity to charge a premium price?
- How can we build an enduring reason for preference among customers in each target segment?
- How can we position ourselves as being the best when there are many others to choose from?

In the following case study, BMW shows how understanding consumer thinking and behavior can generate powerful strategies for brand performance and customer acquisition, Hello Kitty study demonstrates how one brand can be made to appeal to many market segments, and Royal Selangor reveals the art of niche branding and marketing.

Case Study 1

BMW IN ASIA
Psychographic segmentation

The Asian car industry is crowded with many brands, of which only a few can be regarded as global power brands. One such brand is undoubtedly BMW. In Chapter 2, we saw that much of the value of a brand is built through the associations people have with them. Consumers can become highly attached to brands and use them as extensions of their own personalities. The key to brand building is to understand the personality of consumers—their self-esteem, hopes and aspirations, motivations, and behaviors. The BMW approach to branding does exactly this. BMW has identified three broad market segments based on psychographic data to which they cater with their 3, 5, and 7 series models.

The least expensive range is the BMW 3 series, and the buyers of this model are characterized as and with:

• young professionals
• high-earnings potential
• active lifestyles
• independent thinkers who are not influenced by peer pressure
• desiring a brand that reflects their own performance

In creating the brand personality and values for the 3 series (based on the buyer characteristics), BMW defined it as:

• youth
• dynamism
• fun
• sportiness

The second market segment, at which the BMW 5 series is aimed, was found to have the following characteristics:

- above 30 years of age
- in middle management and above
- people who relish challenges
- opinion formers among their peers
- looking for a brand that delivers on performance and driving experience, together with the design features of a luxury car

The brand values appropriate for this segment were established as:

- innovation
- professionalism
- individualism

The BMW 7 series segment has the buyer characterized as:

- male
- senior managers or equivalent
- people who have been successful in their chosen professions
- independent
- looking for a brand of car that symbolizes their success, but not one driven commonly by their peers: a sophisticated luxury car that has technological superiority and is a pleasure to drive

The chosen brand values are appropriately

- superiority
- exclusivity
- autonomy

Finding New Customers I
Once it has been identified that key market segments share the same psychographic characteristics, the company can then

search for these types of customers, who may currently be buying products from other companies, and use specific messages to entice them to migrate to its brand.

In one such case, BMW in Singapore was conducting some focus groups as part of its regular program of research, when it discovered a large group of drivers who shared the same psychographic characteristics as BMW 3 series drivers, but were driving Japanese cars. These drivers did not buy BMW as the monthly payment costs were high. The challenge was to somehow reduce the cost without a downmarket promotion scheme that could damage the BMW image. The solution was an innovative finance scheme called "the balloon payment." Monthly payments were reduced to below the psychological barrier of S$1,000, with the customer paying a lump sum at the end of the seven-year loan. This scheme was new to the country, and thus, seen as relevant and appropriate to BMW as innovation is one of the brand's core values.

To introduce the scheme, the communications strategy had to reinforce the brand values without alienating existing customers. The resulting creative proposition of "Don't Dream, Drive" was successful in attracting new customers without compromising the aspirational nature of the BMW brand. More cars were sold in the three-week promotional period than three-quarters of the annual sales of cars in Singapore, a figure equivalent to 35% of the company's total BMW's leadership positioning.

Finding New Customers II

In the Singapore market, one in 10 cars on the road is a Mercedes-Benz, but BMW discovered that some of the younger Mercedes-Benz owners harbored slight negativity towards the brand. These owners were really more in tune with the BMW image, but had bought Mercedes-Benz cars through peer and parental pressures. The issue here was to persuade them that it was all right for them to buy a BMW. Research showed these drivers were happier conversing in Chinese, and so a Mandarin campaign was run—saying that to demonstrate success they did not have to run with the crowd. Again, the initiative was a success because BMW got into the minds of consumers through psychographic analysis.

Brand strengths: understanding the consumer, brand values, innovation, consistency and appropriateness of marketing communications.

Case Study 2
HELLO KITTY
Branding an idea and
selling it to different segments

Hello Kitty is an idea based on the cartoon character of a small cat that looks kind and cute, has a button nose, two black dot-eyes, six whiskers, and a ribbon or flower in her hair. The cat has no mouth, and this represents a major source of emotional association for buyers, as they can project many different feelings onto the little cat. The owner and the cat can be happy, sad, thoughtful or any other feeling they want to be, together. Hello Kitty is actually 25 years old but has perpetual youth. For Japanese company Sanrio Co, a stationery producer, she has become a major brand success, multiplying profits in the financial year ended March 31, 1998 by thirteen times— during a recession! Adored by many demographic segments of the market, Hello Kitty's main target audience, as expected, is children, but Sanrio says it has now successfully extended the brand to teenage women above 20 years. Hello Kitty has become an icon with global appeal. As the girls, who first bought her when they were young, grow older, they nostalgically buy Hello Kitty products as adults. There are Hello Kitty tea sets, toasters, mobile telephone cases, erasers, motorcycles, mouse pads, spectacles, and other products. For bedtime, there are Hello Kitty pajamas and bedsheets. The company apparently adds 600 new products a month to the 15,000 items or so already available. Hello Kitty has taken Asia by storm, and has 40 stores in the U.S. with subsidiaries in Brazil and Germany.

Sanrio runs Hello Kitty cafes in Japan, and has started to franchise theme restaurants, the first of which is Maxim's Caterers Ltd in Hong Kong, to be opened in late 1999, with more to follow in the year 2000. Franchises in Seoul and Taipei are also on the horizon. Apart from these brand extensions, Sanrio intends to introduce new cartoon characters including a hamster and a rabbit. Financially, the brand has been phenomenally profitable, even during the recession.

Brand strengths: clear understanding of segment needs, application of these to brand extensions, brand consistency.

Case Study 3

ROYAL SELANGOR
A niche-market helps
establish an international brand

Royal Selangor is a corporate brand from Malaysia that has penetrated international markets. The main products in the range of over 1,000 items are decanters, goblets, tankards, and other usable or decorative artifacts made of pewter, such as elegant tea sets, captivating photoframes and handsome desk accessories.

Pewter is a metal alloy comprising pure tin mixed with a small portion of copper and antimony to strengthen it further. Royal Selangor started the pewter industry in Malaysia in 1885, and is proud of its heritage as the leading pewter producer in the world. From the small cottage industry that it was, it now operates the world's largest pewter factory, employing over 500 pewtersmiths.

From its humble beginnings, Royal Selangor products are

now retailed in more than 20 countries, in premium outlets and stores such as Harrods of London, David Jones of Australia, Mitsukoshi of Japan, Illums Bolighus of Denmark, and the Museum of Modern Art Gift Shop in New York. The company has also established its own retail outlets in major cities of the world, including Singapore, Hong Kong, London, and Melbourne.

Royal Selangor's brand platform focuses on

- heritage—of pewter craftsmanship
- authenticity—the real thing, handcrafted
- innovation—of designs
- leadership—the premier pewter company
- international recognition—designs with global/universal appeal supported by international awards

Royal Selangor's tag line is: Malaysia's Gift To The World.

Combining heritage and innovation

A challenge the brand is facing is to achieve the balance between tradition and modernity. It maintained its traditional image of fine handcrafted authenticity, but needs to introduce enough freshness into its product range to keep buyers interested and to grow the customer base and volume sales. It has managed to do this very well by continuing to craft its products by hand incorporating the old with the new.

Innovation successes are reflected in the winning of numerous prestigious awards such as the Formland Prize at Formland Fair, Denmark in 1989, and the Design Plus Award at the Frankfurt International Fair in 1989 and 1991. A team of local and international designers is responsible for the creation of new product lines. Some of them, like the William Morris Wine Accessories range, are inspired by the collections of the Victoria and Albert Museum, London, a range that produced the winner of the 1997 Gift of The Year Award (Licensed Gifts) in the U.K. Similar ranges with enchanting titles such as Leaf Dominica—a range of pewter cigar accessories—and Moods and Memories—depicting flowers in a combination of pewter, crystal and wood. Royal Selangor says it is the love of beauty and the discernment of quality that is the thread that binds its diverse clientele.

Diversification without brand dilution

In the 1970s, the company diversified its business to the design, manufacture, and marketing of 18K gem-set jewelry, 925-hallmarked sterling silver, and hand-painted collectibles in bonded porcelain, under the brand names of Selberan Jewellery, Comyns Silver, and Selcraft respectively. It founded Selberan Jewellery and has built up a quality reputation and a team of qualified gemologists, designers, and craftspeople trained by European master jewelers. Renowned for its beautiful designs, Selberan Jewellery has won more than 20 design awards. The part of the business concerned with silver items was established in 1993 when Comyns, a company dating back to 1645 and one of the oldest and prestigious manufacturing silver- and goldsmiths in the world, was acquired. With it came a treasure trove of tools, molds, drawings, and over 35,000 historical silver patterns. Similarly, Selcraft with its highly skilled artisans, produces beautiful hand-painted collectibles for leading brands in the U.K. and U.S.

There appears to be a good brand fit here in terms of heritage, authenticity, and quality. Royal Selangor has added innovation to the products, but has chosen to maintain the individual company brand names, with endorsement from the parent brand. The new products have not yet enjoyed the same success as the main brand line, perhaps because extending expertise from pewter to silver and gold may not be credible to Royal Selangor's existing customer base, but it is early days yet.

It will be interesting to see how successful Royal Selangor will be at moving into other brand categories, where consumer perceptions, which dwell on prestige, status, lasting value, and instant cashability, are paramount.

Brand strengths: authenticity, heritage, innovation, niche-market leader, international recognition, use of the word "Royal" in brand name.

4

Creating a Powerful Brand Position

WHAT IS POSITIONING?

All forward-looking companies now regard positioning as the core of competitive strategy. As the ultimate aim of any business strategy is to satisfy the customer, gaining a valued position in the minds of customers is essential. Some people argue that branding is really positioning, stating that unless a brand has a position, it has no unique value in the minds of consumers. You can establish a brand personality, and through precise market segmentation identify and reach your target audience. But what links them together is positioning the brand in the minds of that audience. But, what is a position and how do you arrive at a good strategy for achieving one?

The branding process seeks to create a unique identity, for a company, product, or service, which differentiates it from the competition. In Chapter 2, we saw the need for every brand to have a strategic platform as part of its strategic blueprint. One half of that platform is created by carefully formulating a distinct brand personality, which makes the identity of the brand unique. The other half of the strategic brand platform is positioning. Positioning is critical to brand building because it is responsible for projecting the brand identity and creating the perception and image of the brand in people's minds. In other words, positioning is the process of offering the brand to the consumer. It is positioning that makes the brand appear to be different and better than all competing brands. The key points to note about positioning are:

103

- it is a strategic, not tactical, activity
- it is aimed at developing a strategic, sustainable competitive advantage
- it is concerned with managing perceptions
- brand image and reputation are the result of the positioning process

Positioning is strategic not tactical

Positioning is not a short-term tactical activity. It necessitates a thorough understanding of the current and desired images of the brand and those of its competition, and the selection of strategies to change consumers' perceptions and reach a unique position. The main aim of undertaking any positioning strategy is to differentiate your brand from all the others. This can be achieved in the short-term by new products or services and enhancements to those that already exist. But remember that competitors can easily catch up and overtake you in a relatively short time. Positioning tries to negate this situation by creating a lasting image for your brand, an image that is not dependent on product features or other elements that can be copied. The company must have confidence in its ability to satisfy customers in this way over the long-term.

Positioning seeks a sustainable competitive advantage

Because positioning aims at establishing a long-term competitive advantage, the position a brand adopts must be of importance to the target audience. It is no good offering a proposition that is of marginal benefit or significance. Therefore, any positioning strategy used must be based on real brand strengths that reflect a competitive advantage. This is often achieved by the projection of personality and other intangible values. But again the brand has to be capable of consistently performing at least as well as the competing brands.

Positioning is the management of perception

Customers do not understand products and services as well as the companies that produce them. They may not usually be aware of or understand all the features of a product, but they do know in their minds why they like the product. They often think of the product in terms of the benefits they can gain if they buy the product. Some of these benefits, as we have seen earlier, are intangible as opposed to being tangible. Whether intangible or not, these benefits are real to the customer, whose perceptions tend to focus on them. Customers also discriminate between various alternative choices, and file them away in categories in their minds. These categories or ways in which customers differentiate among brands are called positions. A position is a space the company or brand occupies in the minds of the target audience. Perceptual mapping, examples of which are given in Chapter 6, reveals where a brand's position is relative to positions held by competing brands. It is important to try and secure a position that is distant from those of other brands, otherwise differentiation becomes a problem. To achieve this, a company must have a thorough understanding of *all* the attributes associated with similar brands and the needs they fulfill that appeal to the consumer. Sometimes attributes and needs are not obvious and can only be discovered through research.

Positioning depends completely on creating and managing favorable perceptions. But perceptions of products, services, or companies are often entrenched, and can be difficult to shift. Once a consumer has a bad experience with a product or service, then he or she will be extremely reluctant to try that brand again. Negative perceptions can be changed, but only over a long period of time and with a great deal of effort. If you find out that someone has lied to you, you tend to expect it again from that person in the future, and being told that it will never happen again is usually difficult to believe. Similarly, when a company positions a brand, it is literally making a promise to consumers. If the brand lives up to its promise, the company has a great chance of achieving the brand image it desires, but if it fails to deliver the goods, the brand will suffer from a lack of credibility.

Positioning determines brand image and reputation

This is the importance of positioning. The image and reputation of a brand depends on whether or not it has established a favorable position. For this reason, it must be stressed that positioning should be an ongoing activity. Once a company embarks upon a campaign to achieve a desired positioning objective and to change market perceptions, market communications need to be both persistent and consistent. People are bombarded with thousands of messages every day; the challenge is to keep the brand at the forefront of their minds. Positive associations must be continually reinforced while negative associations must be dispelled. No world-class brand has ever reached a prominent position without a carefully planned, long-term communications strategy.

A consistent, attractive image and an unassailable reputation are not just nice to have, they contribute greatly to the bottom line. Because positioning differentiates a brand from its rivals in a cluttered market by creating a perception of value, the rewards of increased brand equity (referred to in the introductory chapter of this book) are realized, and the company itself draws considerable endurable strength from it.

What is re-positioning?

Most positioning activity is, in fact, re-positioning. Unless a company or product is new, people have already formed judgments about it. In other words, the company or product already has an image, either good, bad or in-between. Many companies are not aware of their exact image, but it is important that image is identified. If a company does not know where it is now, then it is unlikely to get to where it wants to go. Re-positioning has many causes and here are a few of them.

The company or brand has a negative image

This can easily happen and often is not the company's fault. Damage can be done by maverick individuals as in the notorious cases of poisoning of the products, Tylenol and Perrier. It can also be an effect of government policy. If a company builds a highway, for example, and forecasts years ahead the toll charges for the government, the public may know nothing about any intended road price increases until the government announces them at a much later date. This announcement may be handled badly by the government, perhaps being made during recessionary times when disposable income is reduced. Although it is not within the control of the company collecting the toll, it still reflects badly on the company. Not only could this produce a crisis, it could also create a need to restore the image of the company.

Public relations is usually the fire-fighting answer, but forward-looking companies use advertising and public relations strategically to think ahead about potential problems. This is sometimes called scenario planning or issues management. The company looks ahead for a certain length of time—it can be months with fast-moving consumer goods or a couple of decades with conglomerates like ICI—and imagines optimistic, pessimistic, and most likely scenarios that can happen. Based on these readings of the future, contingency plans are detailed for every conceivable situation. A good example of how a company thought about its brand image in this way is seen in Telekom Malaysia's sponsorship of the 1998 Malaysian Everest climb. Many things could have happened including the injury and death of the climbers. But, a comprehensive set of guidelines was prepared for staff covering responses to possible questions the company would be asked in both positive and negative scenarios. Coca-Cola, on the other hand, did not seem to react quickly enough when the European scare surfaced in mid-1999, suggesting that it might not have planned what to say in such unlikely circumstances, and now it has a major re-positioning job to do.

The company or brand has a blurred or fuzzy image

When this happens, people do not feel strongly about image one way or the other, or have mixed perceptions about it. This is quite likely to happen when a brand has not been positioned properly. Perceptual mapping (see Chapter 6 for examples) would probably reveal that the brand is very close to other brands in terms of customer preferences, and so has little to differentiate it. A re-positioning exercise would need to be carried out to get the brand into a space away from the other brands. This may also involve changes to product, packaging, etc.

Competition has moved close or taken over brand position

This is a constant threat facing any successful brand because everyone wants to emulate success. It sometimes takes companies by surprise, as Japanese brand Lexus did to BMW in the U.S. This is a constant hazard in the consumer-goods category. Companies have to be prepared to constantly innovate with existing products and bring out new products to surround their category space. FedEx, one of the world's leading courier companies, upon finding out that all other Asian courier companies had positioned themselves around the benefit of speed, as it had done, moved away with a very large advertising campaign suggesting that whatever the adverse circumstances, FedEx would deliver. It has not lost the speed benefit because this is product-related. It has instead added a dimension of corporate personality to strengthen overall company image, hence differentiating it from the rest of the crowd.

The company embarks on new strategic direction

When a company embarks on a new strategic direction, moves into a new industry, or introduces a brand that is remote from the core business, brands with an already powerful image faces less of a problem this might bring. However, weak brands will find it essential to re-position itself to convince the target audience of its credibility. Dunhill has re-positioned itself away from cigarettes and into fashion apparel, and Coca-Cola feels confident enough to bring out its own brand of clothing. There are limits to brand extensions—if the brand name is not too elastic, a totally new brand name may be necessary.

The company introduces new brand personality

When a company introduces new brand values or personality characteristics, or revitalizes itself, it needs to undertake re-positioning. This is an interesting issue for companies in Asia. Privatization and deregulation have forced many government institutions to change their practices, values, and their cultures. This is a significant challenge, as consumer perceptions are deeply entrenched, and re-positioning requires considerable persistence and repetition, backed up by a totally different brand culture and customer experience. Similarly, re-packaging a brand requires re-positioning. When Raffles Hotel in Singapore underwent comprehensive renovation, it had to be re-positioned as a changed entity without losing the heritage value. Raffles Hotel has a colonial heritage and is named after Sir Stamford Raffles, a former governor of Singapore. It was a renowned hotel where famous personalities and writers like Somerset Maugham had stayed, has its own original drink called "the Singapore Sling," and the famous Long Bar, which was the longest in the country. It underwent an immense transformation to an upmarket image while retaining hotel status. The hotel has only suites available, and has many major brand boutique shops for the affluent— only the rich can afford to stay there. However, it has kept a writers' room with exhibits from famous people, and a snooker room, plus the Tiger and Long Bars, although not as originally sited or designed. And it still serves "Singapore Sling" apparently made to the original secret recipe. Tradition and modernity exist side by side.

The company addresses a new target audience

Moving to a new market segment in addition to the existing ones is always tempting for brand development. The danger lies in alienating the brand's existing customer base. For example, an established and famous magazine brand for women has a current readership of 25–40-year-old women, but wants to extend the brand's customer base down to 18-year-olds. The rationale, of course, is to capture the younger population and get them to stay with the magazine as they grow older. However, 18–25-year-old women have different interests and attitudes, and this presents the re-positioning challenge. How can you change the brand enough to entice the new readership and not lose current readers? Another example is presented by Toyota, which said it is considering joining the Formula One racing by 2003. It is trying to revitalize its image to appeal more to the youth, a segment that tends to buy more innovative products such as those produced by Honda. By joining Formula One it hopes to send a message to young people about the fun of driving, and position Toyota as technically up to date.

Always remember that re-positioning takes place *only* in order to make improvements to the existing perception people have of the brand. Whatever the reason, and however it is done, re-positioning must incorporate an enhancement of the customer experience of the brand.

STRATEGIES FOR BRAND POSITIONING AND RE-POSITIONING

There are many strategies for positioning brands, and many of them can be formed into powerful combinations. The various positioning strategies are based on:

- features and attributes
- benefits
- problem-solving
- competition
- corporate reputation and image
- target user
- cause
- aspiration
- usage
- value or price
- personality
- emotion

Features and attributes

This strategy is a clear candidate for positioning products, and even services. People constantly look at features and attributes, but producing unique and sustainable features and attributes is rather difficult. A feature could be an ingredient that another washing powder does not contain, or the windscreen wipers on the headlights of a car. However, from both of these examples, we can see that features and attributes are not really sustainable in the long-term. Although they may yield a short-term competitive advantage, they are unlikely to be totally and indefinitely unique.

Positioning using this strategy can be advantageous though, as Volvo proved with the safety dimension associated with its cars. The strategy is also a good one for innovative companies like V-Tech, which constantly produces goods with innovative features. A company can get to own a position of market leadership with an innovative features approach.

Benefits

Closely connected to the features and attributes strategy is the benefits positioning strategy. This strategy positions the brand by stressing the benefits of possessing it. Procter & Gamble's shampoo called Head and Shoulders, does not just clean hair but contains the benefit of ingredients that help control dandruff. Phileo Allied Bank's virtual-banking kiosks offer the benefits of multi-transactions together with convenience of not having to go to a branch. Consumers like to have the benefits made clear to them, as often the demand for a product or service is derived from the accompanying benefits accruing and not the features themselves.

Problem-solving

This can be a powerful positioning strategy, as everyone faces problems of one sort or another. Brands that solve problems for consumers are appreciated. IBM's entire corporate positioning is now centered on the execution of this strategy, even down to its tag line of "Solutions for a Small Planet." Instead of marketing computer hardware, it is now marketing integrated solutions to clients' IT problems. Sometimes the solutions strategy is related to the benefits strategy. Eye Mo, for example, offers the benefit of caring for your eyes, and also helps to prevent the eye strain associated with long-distance travel.

The problem-solving positioning strategy requires a full under-standing of consumer needs and well-trained staff with the appropriate social and communications skills, especially in the service industry.

Competition

Positioning against the competition has to be handled with care, from legal and an advertising standards perspectives. This strategy is employed with new product launches for beverages, taste tests being an example. Pepsi used this positioning against Coca-Cola some time ago. Service standard positioning is also typical of this strategy, with one company claiming the best customer service. Others aim to impress upon people that they are aiming to get that top spot, as Avis does with its "We try harder" positioning. Avis, by admitting it was number two, made life very difficult for the number three. Benchmarking studies allow companies to assess their competencies against the best in their class. Claiming the top position is good if it can be sustained, or if it is a unique product or service that perhaps creates a new category. Companies with the brand characteristic of innovation sometimes use this strategy to promote this position.

Another aspect of competitive positioning is claiming the top spot through innovation. If a company can do this consistently, it is regarded as a market leader, as is Amazon.com, even though a competitor claims it sells more books on-line.

Corporate reputation and image

The existing brand reputation and image can be a good choice of positioning strategy, and house or endorsement branding adopts this route. It is often successful with big brands because they usually target the same market segments to which they are already selling products. This strategy is usually a supportive one, in the sense that each product or service will endeavor to create its own brand positioning, but adding considerable strength to whatever is chosen. Procter & Gamble, famous for developing product brand positioning, is now starting to globally support some of its individual brands with the parental seal of approval.

Another example of this is Farley's, the baby food producer. The company was bought by Heinz in 1994. Since then, brand positioning has moved away from being product-specific to focus more on the Farley name, and with products such as Farley's Baby Milk, there is co-advertising with Heinz baby products using the slogan "Farley's and Heinz for every little step." There is double value here with the power of two companies famous for their baby foods.

Target-user

Target-user positioning makes sure that the brand has clear positioning for each specific target audience it addresses. This is a strategy that can be used in two ways. One way may be described as one brand having many faces if there is a multi-segment audience. It is typically used by brands with line extensions, like Nike, Reebok, and Adidas in the training-shoe market. There is a generic corporate brand positioning but individual products aimed at specific sports users are targeted with appropriate sponsorship and endorsement deals. The second way of using this strategy is to find a specific segment and giving it precisely what it wants, for example, instant noodles for people who do not have the time, inclination, or opportunity to cook a meal.

Cause

Cause-related marketing is a fast-growing part of corporate advertising and promotions, and some agencies have created a new consultancy division just for this specialization. The strategy here is to ally the company with a worthwhile cause, which will not only strengthen the company's image in general, but will also attract and retain customers who identify themselves with that particular cause. The Body Shop is the most frequently quoted example for this type of strategy. Its positioning is that of a radical business, challenging norms, and celebrating the power of the individual, while being socially conscious and committed to the community. The Body Shop prides itself as being a value-driven company, and constantly tries to improve its impact on the communities in which it trades and the world we live in. It even publishes a Values Report evaluating its performance on social, environmental, and animal protection issues—its causes.

Cause positioning is very much a long-term strategy—once a company has identified itself with a cause, it cannot opt out of supporting it quickly. A large amount of investment may also be required to support various activities associated with the cause.

Advocates of this positioning strategy claim that companies which adopt this strategy are building up a store of consumer goodwill that could be extremely useful in times of crisis. As a company gains power, it also gains more close investigation of its activities, and helping a good cause might offset any negative associations that might arise. It can also be argued that as brands become closer on other positions such as price and quality, cause-related positioning offers them a real point of differentiation, as a company can "own" a particular cause. A 1998 survey of marketing directors revealed that 58% of them agreed that this strategy provides companies with a good opportunity to address business objectives and social issues at the same time. In terms of results, it can be amazing. The Body Shop sells a product every 0.4 seconds, has over 86 million customers worldwide, offers a range of over 800 products and accessories, trades and operates in 47 countries in 24 languages, spanning 12 time zones, with over 1,600 outlets globally.

Aspiration

Aspirations are ambitions, cravings, desires, dreams, goals, hopes, longings, and wishes. They thus provide some excellent scope for positioning brands. In an earlier chapter, we saw that people have their own self-concept about who they are and who they want to be, and that they gravitate naturally towards brands that can help them to express their aspirations or link them to their hopes and dreams in some way. Aspirations are omnipresent. When people travel, they always wish they were staying at the better standard hotel down the road. When they drive their cars, they are always looking at the vehicle next to them, to see if it is a superior model. Improvement is a natural human want, and brands provide the opportunity to satisfy this part of our nature.

Luxury brands like Cartier give people the chance to express their success. Fashion brands such as Gucci give people the chance to belong to an exclusive club. The point to remember about aspirational positioning though, is that there are those who can buy prestige brands and there are those that can only dream about buying them. Marketers have to insure that they address both types of people.

Usage

How and when consumers use products can help companies to position their brands. Coffee, for example can be positioned as a drink to

- relax and unwind after a hard day's work
- comfort and soothe when faced with a problem
- energize and give a lift when feeling jaded
- be part of a social group by having a morning coffee with your friends
- express sophistication by consuming a special brand
- be part of a ritual while organizing one's work for the day

Value

Value has several meanings to different people. For some, it means price, and in this context, the pricing of brands relates to value for money. Value for money implies a combination of price and quality, however. If

Burger King products tasted dreadful, a low price would not compensate. But a low price with consistently acceptable quality makes for a good brand. This brand-positioning strategy requires cost leadership, or the ability to be one of the industry's lowest-cost producers. Brands are not made through price wars and discounting. That approach leads to commodity status in consumer thinking and positioning purely on price is extremely difficult to defend.

A value-positioning strategy can also be achieved by appealing purely to quality and emotional value. Disneyland has succeeded in doing this by combining a good combination of price and quality with fun and lasting memories.

Personality

Positioning based on personality can be the most powerful of all the strategies if correctly formulated and executed. The creation of a personality for a product, service, or company has been discussed comprehensively in Chapter 2, but the basis behind the strategy is to project personality characteristics as part of a brand's identity, which people will find attractive. The personality may contain characteristics similar to those possessed by the target customer group, or those which they aspire to have or be with.

Emotion

This positioning strategy is often used by companies either on its own or in combination with other strategies. It is powerful because emotion sells, as any advertising executive will tell you. It appeals to the right side of the brain, but sometimes requires the inclusion of an appeal to the rational, logical side of consumer thinking in order to attract enough of the target population. Emotion is very strong in every individual even though emotional feelings may sometimes be repressed, as they tend to be in Asia compared to the U.S., for example. No company can afford to ignore the power of emotion in creating or strengthening its position through marketing communications, and the general trend in advertising is now much more inclined to emotional ways of imparting messages than it was a few years ago. In trying to project an identity that will generate an image of respect and admiration, emotion will be an inevitable and important aspect of total positioning strategy.

Around the world, emotion is having more impact on positioning. Even producers of white goods, such as washing machines, are realizing the importance of emotion in positioning their products. Michael Treschow of Electrolux AB said, "We need to have more passion for products," when announcing a plan for a range of colored household appliances, adding, "Washers and refrigerators should have attitude and personality." The series of Singapore Telecom (SingTel) television commercials using humor with Ringo the parrot was good. One of them showed Ringo getting into an aggravated state and then nodding off to sleep on its perch—the parrot was waiting for its owner to get off the telephone so it could use it and talk to some friends, thereby illustrating humorously the benefits of having a second fixed line (and the frustrations of a family not having one). The Banyan Tree Resorts and Hotels really understands the value of romantic, sensual emotion, and is growing the brand through this positioning strategy (a case study of how the company does it follows at the end of this chapter). The Asian Home Gourmet case study also illustrates how emotion can be brought into basic products with style and creativity. Sex, music, aspirations, nostalgia, humor, and many other communications techniques are used in appealing to the emotional drive of consumers. But bear in mind that the interpretations of emotional imagery may vary from country to country.

Combinations of positioning strategies

Companies have learnt to harness the power of positioning by using a combination of two or more positioning strategies. Some naturally go together like aspiration and emotion, bringing intense feeling into advertisements. Nike's "Just do it" campaign used combination to great effect, adding personality in also with sports heroes. Cause and emotion also fit together naturally as used by Benetton, for example. Features and benefits are so close that they inevitably combine.

The new range of organic cosmetics marketed under the brand name, Lush, newly arrived in Asia, is an interesting example of positioning combinations. It is number one in so much as it is sold as foods are in supermarkets, and laid out as grocery-store products are. Supermarket-type baskets are there for you to pick up the Lush products you want. Combining this with features and benefits, the products are freshly made by hand and have shelf-life dates, which demonstrates the freshness to the consumer. To suit the lifestyle and emotional elements, they are made only from organic ingredients. Products in the range, such as soaps and shampoos, are given a dash of personality with names such as Jumping Juniper, Summer Blues, and Pineapple Grunt, and solve consumer problems with ease of selection. Finally, by avoiding expensive packaging and allowing customers to choose amounts—you can scoop some up just like ice cream—Lush represents value. All the products look like foods to eat—like cheeses, pate, desserts—a truly number one brand that has created a new category.

The case study on the Asian Home Gourmet brand in Chapter 7 demonstrates how a good combination of positioning strategies can be achieved. It should be mentioned, however, that wherever possible emotion should be included in some form, because successful positioning usually influences both the heart and the mind. For example, Volvo had one advertisement for its C70 model that appealed to both the rational and emotional sides of the brain, by saying boldly, "Think like an accountant, act like a sportsman."

Positioning brands for equality and superiority

Another component in the strategic positioning equation is the need for a company to consider what it is trying to achieve with respect to its competitive set. Of course, the very nature of positioning means that it is trying to influence people to think that its brand is different and better than the rest of the market category alternatives. But within that context, the company needs to consider both its present market position, and the long-term position it wants its brand t_ gccupy.

If the company is a new or late entrant to the market, or has found that its position is behind that of its competitors, then its positioning strategy may aim merely for achievement of equality with respect to the competition. Its aim will be to convince the target audience that it is just as good as other brands. In this situation, the company may have to concentrate on strategies based on features and benefits, value for money, and usage to manage consumer perceptions in order to create a quality image, one of legitimacy.

On the other hand, as an established, the company might want its brand to be the undisputed leader, the preferred choice. This is no easy task, especially since it is extremely difficult to maintain any kind of sustainable competitive advantage with traditional positioning strategies such as features and benefits. In cases like these, personality and strategies based on emotional and aspirational associations are more appropriate. Prestige and luxury brands are typical examples.

The point is that the brand's vision and goals, together with the choice of target market segments, will have profound implications for positioning strategy, and it is therefore vital that these aims are clearly defined.

How many positions can a brand have?

Positioning is the outward expression of a brand, and the reality therefore is that a brand can only have one true position. As positioning presents the identity and personality of the brand to the outside world, a multiple personality would seem odd at the very least, and at worst, schizophrenic. Consumers make brands famous for many reasons, of which the most important is that they come to trust brands as friends. This is why deciding on the brand-positioning strategy is such an important part of brand strategy. However, there are ways in which the brand may be presented differently to various target audiences. The success of this depends on an accurate judgment of the segments that exist in the market, and the segments' precise needs and wants.

For example, a chocolate-based drink may have a central positioning of nutrition. This could be presented as an energy-giving drink for active people, a dietary supplement for the elderly who have trouble eating many solid foods, an essential growth supplement for youngsters, and a relaxing drink for tired people before they go to bed. By appealing to these various segments, we have not stepped away from the central positioning.

Positioning is wasted without the brand experience

Positioning is the persuasive part of the strategic brand platform. Because positioning is strategic in nature, it is long-term and not normally changed, except for the re-positioning reasons described

earli
diffe
upon
posit
of so
irrep
comp
bran
to ins
comp
be co
the b
cover
everyc
values

Positi

Positio
therefo
market

120

written briefs for internal and external purposes,
representation of the brand is carried out with
These briefs usually take the form of positi
describe the position the brand is to take
should, therefore, be written in a
understand, minus technical or org
not written for distribution t
documents prepared to assi
position into accurate cr
of voice to suit the p
many companies
result, adverti
desired eff
Posi

as teenagers or rich people, then it would be most appropriate for the company to adopt a standard positioning, the way brands such as Nike and Rolex do. They have consistent advertising, promotion, and key messages around the world. However, if segments differ from country to country, then different positioning strategies will be required with different messages. Some brands can also be perceived differently by people in different countries. So, while a brand of beer is perceived as average in one country, it may be regarded as a prestige drink in another. This situation often relates to the country or region of origin, a factor that is discussed in Chapter 7. But, the point is that different positioning is required to maximize the market opportunities.

Positioning statements: What they are and why they are needed

Positioning is critical to business success, but its effectiveness in managing the perceptions of various target audiences depends on marketing communications. There is, therefore, a need to produce

...o insure that any
...absolute consistency.
...oning statements, which
...in people's minds. The briefs
...language that consumers can
...nizational jargon, even though it is
...o the public. The briefs are internal
...t advertising agencies interpret the brand
...ative copy with the appropriate style and tone
...rsonality of the brand. It is astonishing to find that
...do not bother to script positioning statements. As a
...ing and other communications often fail to have the
...ct, and money is wasted.
...ioning statements should convey the following information.

- The brand—state the name of the brand, and follow it by the words "is better than" to remind the company that this is what the statement is intended to convey!
- The brand's target market segment(s)—prepare a positioning statement for each target segment if the brand has more than one. Sometimes, for corporate branding purposes, a master brand statement is written with individual statements for sub-brands, like subsidiaries. Whatever the situation, define each market segment as clearly as possible.
- The competition—describe the nature of the competitive set. Focus on this clearly. For a product, this would mean specifying the category within which the brand is competing. Think of and name the direct competitors.
- The key competitive advantages—spell out why the brand is different from, and better than, the other brands in the competitive set. Mention a USP (unique selling proposition) if there is one.
- The key results—indicate the way by which consumers will receive a better experience when they interact with the brand—the sustainable benefits that consumers will gain from associating with the brand as opposed to other brands.

A positioning statement has greater power and is more effective if it includes the brand personality characteristics or values. First, it will form a substantial part of the brand's competitive advantage, and second, it will remind advertising and promotion agencies as well as the company's staff to include it in their suggestions for marketing communications. The brand characteristics or values should fit in with the wording of the previous two sections of the positioning statement. Avoid vague terminology such as "satisfying customer needs" or "superior quality." These may mean something to the company, but may not be understood by agencies or by the public if they are placed in advertisements and promotional materials. Such phrases or words are frequently used by companies that customers get tired of hearing or seeing them.

Lastly, when preparing the positioning statement, remember to exclude anything that is not achievable (or which the customer cannot experience), as this will lead to a lack of credibility.

Case Study 1 illustrates how positioning is an ongoing process. Taking your eye off the competition can be fatal. Southern Unit Trust was wise not to make this mistake, instead it closely monitored its competitors' positions and changed its own position when the competitors came too close. The result—unique differentiation that stays fresh.

The Volkswagen case study describes the huge challenges the company faced when movig into more prestigious markets. And Ikea is detailed as a good example of how to use multi-positioning to establish a market niche.

Case Study 1

SOUTHERN UNIT TRUST
When is a unit trust not a unit trust?
Establishing a position and re-positioning
when the competition follows

Southern Unit Trust (SUT), a wholly owned subsidiary of Malaysia's Southern Bank Berhad, was launched in 1995 with one with fund and one of the youngest management teams for a financial institution in Asia. The small team of 13 had given considerable thought to how it could differentiate their company from dozens of other already established unit trusts in Malaysia. It had a very ambitious vision, which was not an unusual one for any aspiring company: "To become a world-class unit trust management company." The brand values established are:

- professionalism
- trustworthiness
- innovation
- consistency
- world-class standards

SUT consistently strove to achieve world-class standards by benchmarking against the world's best in the industry. However, it quickly realized that to make any impression on an already crowded domestic market place, it had to focus on efforts that would allow the company to stand out from the crowd. This was the challenge the team set themselves, thereby shaping the mission of the company. Defining a position in people's minds posed a problem because customers did not really understand unit trusts.

Research made it clear that to be able to serve customers in a professional way, SUT would have to supply them with accurate and unbiased information on the nature and value of investing in unit trust funds—not just from SUT but from any company. SUT did this by publishing weekly columns called "Wise Moves" in magazines and newspapers, and getting involved in television and radio programs. Through all these activities, SUT reached a wide range of people who tend to get ignored as serious investors in the capital market, namely, young executives, junior staff, women, and senior citizens. The response from these market segments revealed that the need for information was real among those contemplating or approaching retirement, and those who had already retired.

It was at this stage that the focus of the business was decided upon, and the company mission became: "Making Retirement Easier." The company ran weekly seminars on financial planning for retirement, studied more about the people's fears of retirement, and how it could help free them from financial worries. Innovative print advertising and promotion together with continued public appearances at helpful seminars gained SUT the position in the industry and among the population as "the Retirement Specialists." In consumers' minds, it was no longer a unit trust and were trusted. The perceptual leap had been made, and SUT went from strength to strength. The publication of SUT's book, *Wise Moves to Retirement* cemented its market position beyond all doubt.

It took competitors two years to catch up in terms of re-orienting their staff, products, and promotions to close the lead SUT had gained with these market segments. The task for SUT now is to re-position itself, and move away from the competitors who are closing in. SUT is doing this by focusing on the second half of their mission and the word "easier."

SUT has defined what this means in customer terms. Not only is the company producing strategies to make this happen, including web-site trading, but every member of its staff is now applying the five brand values to their jobs to contribute to the goal. By taking this step now, SUT will continue to stay ahead of the pack. The market map in Figure 6 shows the direction the company has moved in relation to competitors.

Brand strengths: living the vision, mission, and values; focus; problem-solving positioning combination; understanding the emotional and rational customer needs of special segments.

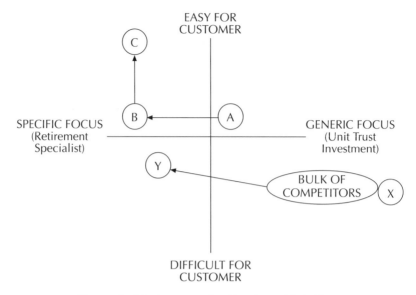

Figure 6: Market map for Southern Unit Trust.

Legend:

X: When SUT entered the market late, the majority of its competitors were already at point X. Hence, SUT was largely undifferentiated, and seen purely as a unit trust investment company with little public understanding.

A → B: SUT, after research with customers and upon having learnt from the mistakes of its competitors, enters at point A, and quickly moves to point B, thereby establishing ownership of the retirement-specialist position.

Y: The competition gradually moves across to point Y seeing the success of SUT's position. But being mainly large and inflexible, the competitors still have not got as far as giving customers a good brand experience.

B → C: SUT now focuses all its efforts on retaining its retirement-specialist position with value-added products, and is moving to point C by applying its brand values.

Case Study 2

VOLKSWAGEN
Changing perceptions and positioning — stretching a brand

Volkswagen (VW) is a famous international brand that has traditionally been associated with the mass market, its most famous model being the Beetle. However, the company is now attempting to move into the prestige- and luxury-car segments, which are dominated by established brands like Mercedes-Benz and BMW. Its first venture into these market segments was with the new Passat V6 Syncro, which is out of the price range of the typical VW buyer. Evidently, other models are planned at higher-level segments and prices. Even though VW owns Audi, Bentley, and Lamborghini, among other brands, many people are skeptical that it can stretch its own brand upwards, as consumer perceptions still associate the VW-branded cars with smaller and less prestigious vehicles. Its "badge value" (brand associations) would not appeal to customers of BMW, Mercedes-Benz, or even Audi. Additional problems arise when consideration is given to the fact that other brands such as Volvo and Toyota's Lexus are also shifting their position to target the prestige market that demands performance, luxury, and marque. VW acknowledges the issues but says it will give customers more products. But is product what the luxury-car owners are really buying? According to research, it is more likely that status, prestige, and self-expression determine customer decision. VW will need to do a considerable amount of consumer-perception management and distributor education to successfully bring any of its VW-branded models into that league.

Case Study 3

IKEA
Using multi-positioning to establish market niche

Ikea is a good example of a company that successfully uses a combination of positioning strategies that satisfies the needs of a particular segment to find a distinctive international position in a competitive market. Ikea is a Swedish company that retails furniture around the world. It uses demographic and family-based segmentation to target primarily young people who cannot afford to buy expensive furniture, but have aspirations for a nice, fashionable and comfortable home. Ikea uses consistent brand visuals both outside and inside its stores, and carefully considers the needs nˆ its market segment by keeping its costs low yet providing good service

For example, it limits sales staff, but provides enough well-trained staff who can answer all questions about the sections to which they are attached. It is supported by an effective computerized system that informs customers of stock and delivery times. Smaller items can be purchased immediately while larger ones take 6–8 weeks to deliver. Customers pay at a final-pay station, and order or select goods as they move through the well sign-posted store. So it appears like a giant supermarket with staff in attendance. Customers can assemble all items themselves as Ikea designs its furniture for self assembly, or has delivery staff to do it for a small additional fee. Furniture is displayed in a room format so that customers can see how various combinations would appear together in their own rooms. Finally, there is a children's play area and a cafeteria catering to those extra needs of young families, and opening hours cater to working customers. In terms of combining positioning strategies, the targeted segment gets value for money, aspirational satisfaction, complete access to varieties and combinations of product features and attributes, rooms that solve choice problems, and emotional satisfaction through thoughtful layout and services.

Brand strengths: accurate segmentation, multi-positioning strategies, category leader.

5

Brand Management

WHAT IS BRAND MANAGEMENT?

Brand management seems a straightforward phrase and was a fairly straightforward job a decade or two ago. But in today's business world, besides being vital to the company's share price, profitability and asset value, brand management can be immensely complex. One reason for this is the dynamic nature of today's world markets.

The job of brand manager has been likened to that of a high-powered team manager or coach (e.g. Brian Epstein of the Beatles, Sir Alex Ferguson of Manchester United) who

- orchestrates the future progress of the team
- plans ahead for development, growth, and shareholders' returns while insuring outstanding short-term results
- motivates everyone involved with the teams' performance
- outmaneuvers the competition
- insures that paying customers get the best possible experience all the time

These duties of a brand manager are similar. However, the role and importance of brand management have changed in recent years. The following are some important changes that have taken place.

Focus shifted from product to customer: Customer-relationship management

Brand managers used to be caretakers of products, which were created by what the company *thought* consumers wanted and not what the market actually wanted. Consequently, brand managers were treated like glorified sales people, but with the additional responsibility for advertising and promotion. Nowadays, there is no doubt that customers play a part in determining the success or failure of a brand. This has resulted in several research studies being conducted at all levels of brand management, including new product development, to determine what is in the customer's mind. In spite of this, there is an amazing number of companies in Asia that still adopt the old approach, which differentiates very minimally between the roles of marketing and sales.

Still, the recent change in focus is so pronounced that some companies, which manage the huge powerful brands, have appointed customer-relationship managers who are responsible for attending to the needs of specific market segments, rather than for a portfolio of products. Segmentation is becoming more important.

Focus changed from product to market: Market and category management

The recent shift in focus to the consumer has driven brand management to taking a market-driven approach, in the sense that companies are often no longer tied to one industry. Brands are no longer treated as products but as markets. Brand management can, therefore, take a cross-industry approach. This is also seen explicitly in the move from product to category management, where certain companies concentrate on dominating market categories that may contain a range of products. In this case, brand management is responsible for category profitability.

Focus shifted from local to global brands: International-brand management

Building world brands is now the ambition of many companies that have already reached successful international status. Acer Computer, for example, is very successful in Asia, but yearns to become a truly global brand. British Airways also desires to be one of the world's most admired and top-rated megabrands. Brand management in such circumstances involves developing corporate strategy at the very highest level and the management of a complex combination of international markets.

From product profitability to total product performance: Brand-equity management

By far, the most important change in the nature of brand management is the attention companies are paying to brand valuation. In fact, some companies appoint brand-equity managers whose sole responsibility is to research and measure brand equity, leaving the marketing aspects of the brand to others. The value of a brand is no longer simply the annual contribution to corporate profits, but the valuation of total brand equity. Furthermore, the total portfolio of brands can add substantial asset value to the value of the company itself. This change has also been partly responsible for the shift from product-brand management to corporate-brand management, since the corporate brand name can amass tremendous value.

The management of brands can obviously be quite wide-ranging, and different companies use brand managers in different ways. Some are assigned to manage just one brand, others to manage a brand range, and yet others to manage a brand category. Some brand managers have global marketing responsibilities while others manage brand-equity growth. The most important issue is to insure that the brand is protected. This guardianship role is discussed in further detail in a later section within this chapter. In the meantime, here are some other perspectives on brand management that concern companies.

REVITALISING BRANDS

Sometimes brands get tired and look old, just like people, and brand managers wonder what they can do to inject a new lease of life into their brands. Brands can lose their potency, but there is no Viagra pill for brands! So, what can brand managers do to keep a brand fresh and inviting, and sustain a high level of performance?

A new look

One way a company can revitalize a brand is by giving it a fresh look. And the temptation to refresh and revitalize a jaded brand by giving it a new logo is often there. The two options for a change in logo are revolution and evolution. Both have their advantages and disadvantages.

The revolutionary path takes a complete departure from the past, leading to a new logo, along with new visuals and packaging, all signifying new resolve and direction for the corporate brand. This path is rarely taken with products as it destroys recognition and recall. Its disadvantage, from the corporate viewpoint, is the loss of brand equity that has been built over the years by customers and employees buying and becoming attached to the brand through its logo. Cathay Pacific totally changed its visual identity, as did British Airways, but this did not prevent Cathay Pacific from going into the red for the first time in its history, while British Airways faced some resistance from customers and staff for its apparent loss of "Britishness."

The evolutionary route is one where detours are made to update the image of the brand by modernizing its logo and packaging in a more subtle and incremental way. Though minor, the changes can still be innovative while leaving recognition by consumers relatively unaffected. Classic marketing practice adopts this route. Abrupt changes can lose consumer trust, and with corporate changes, can even produce hostile

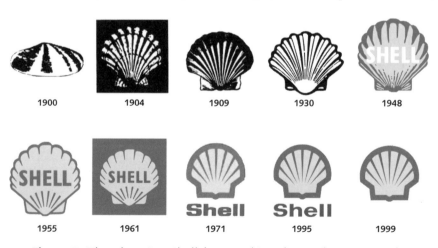

Figure 7: The changing Shell logo—taking the evolutionary path.

Source: www.Shell.com

reaction if consumer experience does not improve. Gradual changes are more readily accepted. A good example of evolutionary change is the Shell logo, which has only appeared in ten forms since its inception in 1897 and is still keeping the scallop symbol. According to Shell, "the scallop, traditionally recognized as a symbol of the sea, reflects our quest and our search for new ideas, new products, and new ways" to serve customers better.

Care has to be taken, especially with products, to minimize consumer misunderstanding when adopting a new look. Tiger Beer of Singapore recently changed its packaging (e.g. colors, logo, etc.), and some customers felt that the product was now not so familiar to them. Customers make friends with brands, and feel they have lost a relationship if drastic visual changes take place. When Pepsi changed to its packaging in order to escape similarities with rival Coca-Cola, the change cost hundreds of millions of dollars in advertising and promotion alone, but appears to have had little effect on sales. So, think carefully before playing around with the visual aspects of a brand. They are recognition factors with a brand's logo or name, and that recognition brings to mind a whole host of emotional associations that consumers have with the brand. Think customer and customer associations.

Brand life cycles and product management

Understanding and using the concept of brand life cycles used to be fairly predictable when the life of a brand was linked to the life of the product or service itself, except for corporate brands. Corporate brands have led the way in proving that brands can have indefinite lives. Top global brands of decades ago still enjoy the same ranking today, and skillfully branded products show no signs of terminal failure nowadays. But this is no accident—brand life can be extended by constant innovation. The motor car is a typical example. The concept of built-in obsolescence is not new. However, the application of brand innovation prolongs the life of a brand. Brand managers, by carefully assessing the market or category conditions, can use the life-cycle concept and innovate before the market reaches maturity, as illustrated in the Figures 8(a) and 8(b), which have been simplified for the understanding of the concept.

(a)

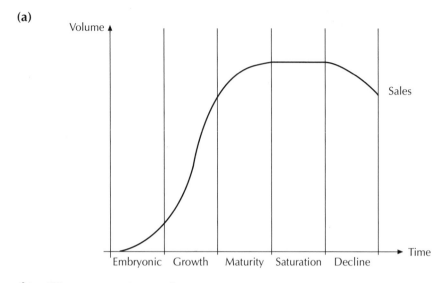

(b) "**I**" represents innovation.

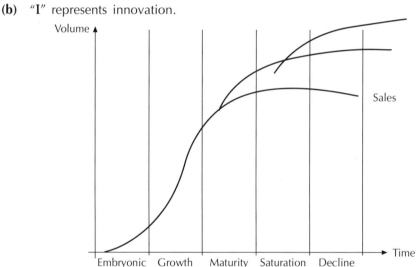

Figure 8: Revitalizing brands by adding innovation
to prolong life cycles.

Figure 8(a) shows the classic life-cycle curve for products and
services. When the new product is introduced, volume of sales is slight
initially, but begins to pick up once market awareness increases. After
this embryonic stage, there is rapid market take-up as demand increases
and other producers come in. This is the growth stage. The market then
reaches maturity as the rate of sales decreases, but supplier competition

remains hot. Saturation follows as new products attract consumers and demand levels off. Sales decline can then follow.

Figure 8(b) shows how a brand can prolong the life cycle, preventing it from going past the maturity stage, and if possible, maintaining the growth phase there. Principally, innovation acts as the catalyst for growth, and companies with solid marketing expertise are able to predict accurately when the growth stage is beginning to fade. It is at this point that they make the decisions to bring in the "facelifts" and new product innovations, usually through features and attributes, and this starts off the growth stage again on its steep climb up.

Asian car manufacturers such as Honda, Toyota, and Nissan are famous for this, changing their model specifications every 18 to 24 months. The increasing skills rate of companies doing this in industries, together with the ability through modern technology to make fast product innovations, have now brought on the need for endless innovation, bigger investment, and at the same time achieving profits. The innovation wheel now turns every six months in the PC industry, but of course, does not turn as fast in industries like foodstuff. So paradoxically, life cycles are shortening, especially in technology-oriented products, but innovation extends and revitalizes the brands. Over time, the product can change significantly, and while it does, the task of the brand manager is to stay with the brand values and retain customer loyalty. The brand manager then has to balance consistency, which is needed for brand building, with change, which is necessary for survival and short-term profits. The message then is "revitalize" but do not "re-valuate."

Brand stretching and extension—How far can you go?

Think of your body. If you try and stretch your limbs now, you may find it a little difficult and it may ache a little, mainly because you are not used to it. Through regular exercise, the stretching will get progressively easier. However, there is a limit to how far you can stretch yourself—beyond which our body cannot take any more. This is generally what happens with brands. A brand has some elasticity as people get used to the brand and like it, and with regular, successful brand management practice, the brand can be stretched in terms of line or brand extensions, but every brand has its limit.

Brand extension occurs when a company uses its brand name to move into a totally new product or service category. Coca-Cola, which diversified into clothing, is a good example of brand extension. A line extension, on the other hand, is where the company uses the brand name to produce a new product or service that is in the same category, even though that category may be broad. The new Jaguar S series could represent this kind of extension, as it is in the same broad category, but some would argue that sports cars are in a category of their own. Deciding what is included in (or excluded from) a category is sometimes difficult. The launch of Pepsi One is another extension, but is it in the soft-drink category or the diet-drink category? Whatever the decision, it is important from an overall brand perspective that both brand and line extensions should carry the core values of the original brand.

The limits for brand or line extension depend on various factors, but basically they boil down to whether or not the consumer will accept the extension or not. Coca-Cola is now stretching its brand past the bottled water phase, which appears to be a reasonable brand fit to the consumer, as it is in the soft drinks business, and into the world of fashion, with two clothing lines under the label, Coca-Cola Apparel. The two clothing lines are called Ware and Threads. Ware is to be targeted at the specialist sports buyer, while Threads is targeting the fashion buyer with jeans and casual clothing. The rationale for this move is that the company wants to be seen as a fashion brand with its clothing extension, which will help the brand connect with its customers in a broader way. In addition, Coca-Cola strongly believes that it has a relationship with the brand that goes beyond drinking, a relationship which it wants to express. Both clothes ranges will be tested in the U.K. and the Irish Republic and distributed under license. It is difficult to predict the outcome of this brand extension. No doubt the company has done its research, but sometimes research can be misleading, as Coca-Cola found out in a previous instance. Even the world's most powerful brand can have its stretch limit, and one cannot help but wonder if that limit has been reached with this brand extension. Virgin has extended into many totally unrelated areas, and not all have been successful. For instance, Virgin Vodka, launched in 1995, has virtually disappeared, and is now available only in duty-free shops. Virgin Cosmetics and Virgin Clothing have also been less successful than some of its other extensions.

Extending prestige and luxury brands

The very nature of prestige and luxury brands means that there are self-imposed limits to brand stretching. Because these brands are positioned in consumer minds as premium status items, extension through reduced quality and a lowering of price is dangerous. It is what these brands mean to people that creates their exclusivity. In marketing jargon, these types of brand are called representational brands. It is fatal to devalue their worth by producing a lower range, which may attract lower-income customers aspiring to own the brand but which simultaneously alienates the core customer base who regard it as an exclusive club. The only viable solution here is to distance the brand from its new offspring by choosing a different name but remaining true to the brand core values. Rolex has done this successfully with its Tudor brand. The advertisements for both are very similar in content, tone, and style, yet one can virtually tell that the products are from the same company, with only their name differentiating them. The DKNY brand has carried out a similar strategy with its differently priced Donna Karan range. For these types of brands, decisions need to be considered carefully because the greater the dilution of quality and prestige, as perceived by customers, the greater will be the negative impact on brand image. Needless to say, advertising and promotion also require careful management.

Extending functional brands

Functional brands are different from representational brands in that they tend to operate at lower price and prestige levels, yet offer the level of quality and effectiveness to do what they are supposed to do. As they are in the lower half of the prestige-status spectrum, the options to move further down or up into the prestige area are somewhat limited. To move down brings the brand closer to commodity status, and may affect the reputation of the existing brands. Attempts to move up can be hampered by lack of consumer confidence for a brand that does not have strong upmarket associations. It is a difficult task to add prestige and status to a brand when it lacks a track record and its company name is associated with less prestigious brands. So, there is little room for maneuver within the spectrum.

Any extensions of functional brands cannot be too far from the original brand. This invites product cannibalization when the extensions and the brand are positioned too closely to each other. The danger is customer confusion—customers cannot differentiate clearly in their minds the various offerings presented. When Thailand's Boon Rawd Brewery's major brand Singha was threatened by a lower-priced competitive brand called Chang from Carlsberg, the Thai brewery introduced its own lower-price and lower-quality brand Leo to stop Chang from taking away a major portion of Singha's market share. However, the position Leo was supposed to occupy in customers' minds took an unexpected turn. Boon Rawd Brewery perceived Leo to be better than Carlsberg's Chang, to the extent that Leo began to compete with its own big brother, taking away sales from Singha. So, Singha ended up with Chang, commanding lowest segment of the market, while Leo commanded some of the lower-middle market. The end-result: Singha lost out to both Chang and Leo.

SEGMENTATION, BRAND STRATEGY, AND PORTFOLIO MANAGEMENT

Managing brands often entails looking after brands that operate in different segments and with different levels of competitive strength. It is worth taking periodical snapshots of the situation that the brand or brands happen to be in. In Figure 9, for example, there are four basic situations.

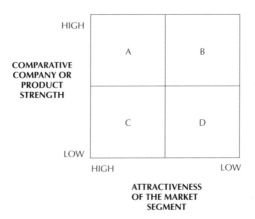

Figure 9: Brand/segmentation matrix.

Situation A: Finding the company or product brand in this quadrant is good news. The brand strategy would be to maintain the strength of the brand in terms of product enhancement or company profitability and image while keeping an eye on the competitors' movements.

Situation B: The top right quadrant suggests a good brand positioned in an unattractive segment. It would be useful to determine how this situation arose—the company may have taken its eye off the market when segment decline occurred. Selection of a suitable strategy needs careful thought, particularly as re-positioning the brand to appeal to another segment may or may not be possible.

Situation C: This quadrant needs some thought. The segment is attractive—probably very profitable, too—but the company or brand is not as well placed as its competition. Possible strategies are revitalizing the brand, re-positioning the brand, product enhancement, or even replacement.

Situation D: When caught in this unfortunate situation, withdrawal is inevitable. The decisions are thus confined to which method is used to exit and the speed with which it is done.

If the brand manager has a portfolio of products, a matrix like this borne out of research, would be even more revealing, especially if the strength of the brands is measured against that of the competition, and the segment growth and profitability are also measured. Some companies position two or three brands in an attractive segment to keep out the competition. Brand strength can be placed on the matrix represented by circle size and competitors by different colors.

MERGERS AND ACQUISITIONS

When involved in the tortuous process of mergers and acquisitions, there are many things to think about, and brands rank among the most important. Usually, there is some synergy between the merging entities, and decisions have to be made about how the brands from the separate entities may compete. The Daimler-Chrysler merger is a good example.

The newly merged, giant car company has made brand separation a key target for the new management, and brand managers have been appointed under the new structure to protect and promote the separate brands. A decision has been taken not to have any Daimler-Chrysler brands, so clear positioning of each individual brand becomes important for brand management. In fact, the two major brand names will not even appear for sale in the same premises.

Mergers and acquisitions also have implications on brand culture, particularly if the company is in the service industry. The importance of brand culture to the consumer brand experience follows.

CO-BRANDING

It is becoming increasingly common to see brands from different companies appearing together in the same campaign or specific communications. A catalyst for this has been the recent recession, because by embarking on joint advertising and promotion campaigns, there is an obvious cost-saving element. However, there can be other advantages as well, such as gaining access to the customer base of the co-branding partner or partners, and building value-added packages for consumers. For example, Coca-Cola, music company Capital Artists, and Henderson Land Development launched a HK$100-million campaign called Red Passion in the hope of getting consumers to buy more soft drinks, music, and hopefully residential properties. Coca-Cola has also teamed up with some book publishers to package books with its diet products. Visa International has a marketing agreement in the Asia Pacific with Yahoo! Inc. to offer on-line shopping. McDonald's teamed up with the owners of Snoopy, the famous cartoon character, where the purchase of a McDonald's Extra Value Meal allowed people to obtain a Snoopy toy dressed in the costume of that country or a U.S. state.

Many more examples can be seen worldwide, but the key question for brand management is whether being associated with other brands represents a good brand fit or not. In other words, a company has to be very sure that the symbiotic relationship will not devalue its brand. Associating with a brand that has different brand values could certainly do this. There is also the question of whether there is a good fit with the respective customer bases. Coca-Cola's association with Henderson Land

Development might have addressed totally different customer bases, but the company associated itself with a declining property market. On the other hand, Coca-Cola's research shows 30% of Diet Coke drinkers read books, so the tie-up with the book publisher might make sense. Visa International and Yahoo! have a good overlap of customer bases, while McDonald's and Snoopy are both providing value for money and fun for families.

The secret to successful co-branding is to stay true to the brand personality and values, and to choose partners carefully—partners who not only share some of those values, but target similar consumer segments to which value-added packages will appeal. Finally, when co-branding, insure that the brand does not get eclipsed in advertising and promotions by the brand or brands with which it is being associated. Insure that the brand gets a good share of mind!

CARING FOR AND PROTECTING BRANDS

The caring for and protecting of brands is often called brand guardianship, brand custodianship, or brand stewardship. It is absolutely vital for brand success. But how to go about it and who should do it?

What can be done?

As seen earlier in this chapter, brands are capable of defying their normal life cycles and living almost indefinitely. However, this would not be the case if the brand is neglected and left unprotected. Constant vigilance is necessary. The basis of brand guardianship is insuring that the brand platform remains intact. This means making sure that every activity connected with the brand personality and its core values is consistent and appropriate, and that the positioning of the brand is not compromised in any way. The aim of the whole process is to provide the customer with the best possible brand experience. The importance of managing and guarding the brand via the communications strategy (dealt with in Chapter 8), is most important. Many companies fail, through brand neglect, and wonder why their image is not up to scratch.

An equally (some would say more) important aspect of brand guardianship is the ability of the company to build a brand culture that reflects the personality and positioning of the brand that appears in the glossy advertisements and other forms of communication. This is critical to companies in service industries, where customer interaction with the brand is more intimate and personal. A special section on how to develop a brand culture for a company follows.

Living the brand—Developing a strong corporate-brand behavior and culture

Companies are judged by their behavior. Everything they say or do affects their image and reputation. In order to build a powerful corporate brand with a corresponding image, the behavior of the company has to be controlled and shaped in such a fashion that people's perception of it is always favorable. This also makes for good customer relationships; corporate behavior perceived in a negative way will give rise to poor relationships. One of the roles of brand guardianship is to manage corporate behavior, and this role is both vital and wide-ranging.

However, to develop a powerful corporate brand image, where the company is the center of attention and where customers interact a lot with the company's representatives, a whole brand culture has to be built around the brand personality.

What is brand culture?

Corporate culture is a much-discussed topic in Asia these days, as companies try to accommodate modern work practices and change management styles. Many sophisticated training and organization-development initiatives are adjusted by internal and external specialists to suit or influence current corporate cultures, and help promote efficiency and effectiveness for the future. Corporate culture in its crudest form is described as "the way we do things around here." Essentially, it is the sum of a complex blend of employee attitudes, beliefs, values, rituals, and behaviors that permeate a company and give it a unique style and feel. Corporate culture can have a profound effect on both staff and customers. For staff, it can provide an invigorating, stimulating, and exciting place to work in, or it can make going to work a dismal daily experience. It can also empower people or enslave them.

Because culture is all-pervasive, it inevitably has an impact not just inside, but outside the organization. Customers who come into contact with staff can feel it through the attitudes and expressions of the staff, and see it in the staff's comments and service standards. Corporate culture can, thus, impact considerably on corporate image in a negative or a positive way.

Corporate image, branding, and culture

When a company tries to develop and maintain a good corporate image, it has to create a suitable culture. If the company is creating and maintaining a corporate brand, then the culture has to be appropriate to the essence of the brand. Corporate branding is, in fact, a very positive and well-received way of changing the culture of an organization, for reasons that will soon be discussed.

When building a new corporate culture or changing the existing one, companies often do this by establishing some corporate values as a behavioral guide for people to follow. The most attractive (and often most successful) way to build a brand is to create a personality for the brand—a personality that summarizes what the brand really stands for. If a brand platform is built through developing certain personality characteristics or traits, then it is easier for consumers to diagnose it, so to speak, and they are more likely to be attracted to it. Once the personality characteristics have been chosen as the building blocks of the brand, the culture of the company then follows that same identity. The personality characteristics then assume the same role as the corporate values.

If the company already has a set of corporate values at the time it embarks on a corporate-branding exercise, then a decision will have to be made whether to keep the existing corporate values, or replace them with the new personality. If the corporate values are somewhat similar to the brand values, then the corporate values can be maintained, and the personality used to reinforce and add more strength to the practice of these values. For example, if the company has reliability as a value, then the personality characteristic of dependability would translate into roughly the same message. On the other hand, if the corporate values are far removed from the brand personality, then there is a choice of discarding some or all of the old values and starting to inculcate a completely new culture based on the new core values of the brand. The company may want to retain some of the old values that are still regarded as important to its future, (e.g. quality); there is no harm in doing so as long as the value does not conflict with the personality. Indeed, some companies have a mixture of conventional values and personality characteristics. Another word of caution here is that too many values will cause confusion among staff, and will be difficult to project consistently as a personality to the outside world.

Defining brand values

It is not good enough to simply select the corporate brand personality characteristics and inform everyone that they now exist. These personality characteristics must be closely defined at two distinct levels.

First, they have to be defined generically at a corporate-wide level, so that employees can see how they fit into the vision and mission of the organization, and understand each characteristic or value. It is important that all employees are informed of the corporate personality and the reason for it, and why the behaviors included in the definitions are so important to the branding process. This step alone calls for substantial awareness and briefing efforts on behalf of the company. This may take the form of short training programs.

Second, the personality characteristics must be defined at the individual level. For a company to brand itself properly, everything it does must reflect the corporate personality characteristics. This means that every employee, from the CEO downward, must attempt to live that personality in the job that he or she does. The reason for this is simple—an employee may understand the new corporate personality and the general descriptions attached to it, but what he or she really wants to know is what it means for his or her particular job. Above all, the customer has to experience the brand through every employee. This is a matter of insuring that staff are not only aware of the corporate personality characteristics and know what each characteristic means, but also that they know how to apply these values to their particular jobs.

So, in the case of a characteristic, such as caring, the company would need to explain through training what this brand value means to a customer-service assistant, a receptionist, an IT manager, a production supervisor, etc. There is no shortcut to brand building, and the more care that is taken, the more successful the brand will be. If one of the brand characteristics is innovation, the company has to be prepared to tell a van driver, a sales person, an accounts clerk, a human resource executive, and every other individual in the company, what each characteristic means for them in carrying out their jobs. Only then will they know what specific behaviors, attitudes, and relationships they should adopt in order to make that personality come alive.

This is no easy task and it has huge implications for human resource management, development, and training of staff. However, if the company gets it right, the rewards can be spectacular. Do not worry about acceptance of personality based values by staff. In my experience, staff take to them very easily, and can understand why these values will differentiate their company from all the rest. Staff see a sense of purpose with a brand personality that they never seem to with other training and project initiatives.

Developing training for brand values

Training is an integral part of achieving good performance on brand values. Briefing staff on the company's brand strategy, and identifying how staff can apply the values to their jobs is, of course, important. But, however well defined the brand values are, staff may need to learn new skills in order to perform well. It is important to look at each value and decide what these skills are. A fruitful way to do this is by analyzing the behavior of staff who have been identified to be performing to a very high standard on one value. Look at critical incidents that have happened to the person when he or she had to bring that value into action; find out what and how the person did it. Also, interview people who knew about the incident. This research can be very revealing, not just in identifying the skills associated with particular values, but also in terms of what the organizational implications are for helping staff bring that value to life. As an example, the following is the results of a series of interviews with the employees of an Asian bank on the value of caring.

Personal skills required	Organizational implications
◆ Showing empathy	Encouraging openness, honesty
◆ Emotional resilience	Strengthening coaching,
◆ Suspending judgment	counseling
◆ Listening	Training in interpersonal skills
◆ Giving positive and	Developing teamwork
negative feedback	
◆ Self-discipline	
◆ Openness and honesty	
◆ Combining formality and	
informality	

In this example, it was found that it was not easy to really care about others (including staff, subordinates, customers, and suppliers). It is an attitudinal-related skill, which goes much deeper than just being friendly, and can be extremely stressful. An intensive coaching and training effort is required if all employees are going to live the value of care and bring the brand personality to life. Yet, it is absolutely critical to corporate vision, mission, brand strategy, and credibility. There is no short cut to building a strong brand.

Developing brand-personality strategies

Just as a product brand would have its own set of strategies, so too would a company trying to establish its corporate brand. Leaving aside positioning (which was dealt with in the previous chapter), corporate strategy should be based around the brand. I have found it useful to ask divisions and departments within companies to produce plans for the short and medium term on how they are going to deliver on their brand values. So, divisions or departments like information technology, finance, research and development, human resources, production, credit control, logistics, and others, have to develop strategic and tactical plans to inform top management of how they intend to implement each brand value. These plans should not contain vague statements of intent, but concrete action plans detailing timing and accomplishment criteria. Once staff get used to developing such plans, the establishment of the corporate brand is easier to achieve and control, and departments will find it easier to define people's jobs more clearly in terms of the brand.

If innovation is a key brand value or personality characteristic, for example, products and services have to be truly innovative, and the company has to insure this, as Gillette does with its policy of having over 40% of annual sales coming from products introduced in the last five years; 3M has 25%. Some companies with this value, like DuPont, put all employees through innovation training, as they believe everyone, from the janitor to the CEO, can come up with good ideas. Kao, the Japanese personal-care-product company, concentrates heavily on innovation. About 2,000 of its 7,000 employees are dedicated to research and development, approximately three times that of Procter & Gamble. Kao's aim is to become a global player, but states it can only achieve this through producing a constant stream of new products to aggressively seize international opportunities.

Disney Corporation has a section called Imagineering, which is devoted to developing innovations for its six divisions—a 2,200-person think-tank. Within this section are highly paid scientists with expertise in fields such as flight simulation, artificial intelligence, cognitive psychology, neuro-anatomy, mathematics, neural networks, and other disciplines. Their task is to create the future where, for example, there will be virtual theme parks, or where children's wishes for a toy can be conjured up on the website. This is an example of a company living its mission of making people happy.

The message, then, is that every brand value or corporate personality characteristic has to be very carefully defined, not just at the corporate level but at the department and job specific level, too. And each one has to be brought to life.

Reward and recognition

Whenever a company introduces a new process, it must remember that however loyal and enthusiastic its employees are, they want to know what is in it for them. In Asia, there is more of an acceptance of power and authority in organizations than there is in the West. Even so, the universal truth is that employees always perform better if they gain some kind of recognition and reward for changing work practices. The acceptance of personality characteristics into corporate culture is usually supportive, but to increase the speed of the process, it is a good idea to think of ways by which employees can gain recognition and rewards.

Reward: It is not unusual now for companies to allocate a certain percentage of their employees' remuneration packages for values performance. The values may be corporate or brand, but companies realize the worth of doing this. General Electric, for example, links 50% of its annual review to this. Performance on values for Toro accounts for 25% of incentive compensation, with Levi Strauss tying in at one-third. The actual financial amount varies with these companies, but it is never treated lightly. To do so would dilute the importance of values recognition. Putting brand values into performance management and appraisal schemes insures that the values are translated into corporate behavior, so that the consumer sees and experiences consistency. This influences perceptions and has a major impact on the brand image of the company. Further, it increases profitability. Harvard Business School research reveals that companies implementing "performance-enhancing cultures" achieve profit growth of several hundred percent more than those that do not.

This book is not about performance management, but it does highlight how every department and every employee can, and should, help manage and guard the brand.

Recognition: It is not only financial reward that can motivate employees to perform well on brand values. Here is a list of ideas that have been tried in Asian companies and have worked well:

- selecting role models who perform outstandingly well on all values
- selecting values performers who perform outstandingly on one or more but not all values
- CEO award
- competition award
- newsletter and magazine recognition
- customer recognition award
- peer group award
- outstanding team award

Brand manuals

Some companies have brand manuals to establish clearly what can and cannot be done with the company's brands. These are usually written with reference to the visual aspects of the brand. The more difficult decisions are those that cannot be prescribed in advance, such as whether a television commercial reflects the brand personality and positioning properly. Often, the danger here lies in delegating this task to a level that is too junior. With high visibility, such decisions must be taken at the top. However, for day-to-day brand management and as a reference for advertising, promotion, and other agencies, brand manuals are essential.

Who is responsible for brand guardianship and management?

The management of a brand is a process filled with daily decisions. Most companies have brand managers responsible for the development and performance of the brand or a portfolio of brands. The brand manager's job is mainly to:

- analyze the market and its activity, including the growth factors of the total market and various market segments within it, and their performance relative to the competition
- insure that the brand platform is maintained and that the brand stays true to its values and positioning
- propose future brand strategy with particular regard to positioning, extensions, and others
- manage the marketing mix—price, promotion, packaging, and so on
- measure the success of brand performance, assess expenditure against volume, profit, and other variables

But, who is really responsible for guarding the brand? This a question most companies new to brand management have to wrestle with. In some companies, little care is taken at all, and activities that impact heavily on customers are taken by default and sometimes unknowingly by junior staff. In others, the decision is a matter of where in the organization the brand management function should sit. In many Asian companies, for example, marketing and corporate communications are totally separate divisions. In some cases, this means that there is no brand management function, and so the brand is represented differently in communications sent out by the two divisions. Brand consistency just is not there.

For any company, large or small, this absence is a serious flaw in its brand-building process—guardianship of a brand must occupy a high priority. This means that brand management must be handled at a very high level. Ultimately, the CEO is responsible. In some of the major brand companies, the CEO or equivalent is the sole or part decision maker on matters of importance, such as whether or not a new product brand will fit in with the corporate brand core values, and even whether television commercials or other high profile activities reflect brand values. In other companies, high level committees are responsible, either at corporate level or product group level. Nestlé appoints "brand champions" to look after a single brand, but whose role is similar to the brand-equity role discussed earlier. These champions oversee all the brand's activities in all of its operative countries. It matters not so much what process is set up to manage the brands, but what matters is that every possible activity or decision, which can influence the consumer experience of the brand or perceptions of it, is subject to stringent scrutiny. This will then insure both consistency and appropriateness, the essential building blocks of brand communications.

The need for consistency in managing brands

However brand management is organized for the company, remaining true to the brand values is critical. It is not enough to leave such important decisions to the advice of agencies, as they have their own interests in mind. There are brand-specialist consultants who can help with this, and assist with agency briefing and monitoring. Companies that operate internationally must give this very careful thought. For instance, if the brand is marketed and sold through third-party distributors and agents, how can the company control the way in which it is presented, advertised, and promoted? It is for this reason that some major brands handle all brand guardianship matters centrally, and appoint one agency worldwide to handle all campaigns. This is all right for large companies, but presents a problem for the smaller ones—and there is no easy answer. Persistent monitoring is essential. For those using franchising and brand licensing as a means for international expansion, contractual detail on brand values, promotion, and performance is also vital.

Brand management is a complex process, and has to be worked at continuously. Two companies that are models of good brand management are Singapore Airlines (SIA) and Banyan Tree Hotels & Resorts. SIA has a difficult job to do in an "open skies" environment, where every player is constantly making product and service improvements. Renowned throughout the world for its quality service, the SIA brand image would not have remained so high without the constant thought and action directed at giving the customer a better experience. This case study shows brand management at work.

Banyan Tree Hotels & Resorts is in a different industry and a niche market, but customer experience again drives the brand. It is the obsession with guarding the brand that has put this name in the premier league of Asian brands.

Case Study 1

SINGAPORE AIRLINES
Managing a famous brand

Singapore Airlines (SIA) has always desired to be the world's best airline, and it has come close to that goal in recent years, in what is now fast becoming a commodity market. SIA was founded in1972 when Malaysia-Singapore Airlines (MSA) split into two: SIA and MAS (now Malaysia Airlines). SIA's latest acquisition of a 50% stake in Ansett, Australia's second largest airline, underlines its global vision. As Deputy Chairman and Chief Executive Officer Dr Cheong Choong Kong said: "Our intention is to become not just an international airline but a global group of airlines and airline-related companies."

SIA's mission statement is as follows:

"Singapore Airlines is engaged in Air Transportation and related businesses. It operates worldwide as the flag carrier of the Republic of Singapore, aiming to provide services of the highest quality at reasonable price for customers and a profit for the company."

In the world of airline travel, SIA has relentlessly pursued the two things that matter to customers—technology and service, and has lived up its brand promise of "a great way to fly."

Customers like to travel with airlines that have a modern fleet because this satisfies their concerns about safety. SIA has always taken the high-tech route and has been among the first few of the world's airlines to buy the latest airplanes and products. Customers also like good service when flying because it is more than just sitting in a seat: it involves booking the flight, checking in, waiting, boarding, spending time in the "tube," disembarking, retrieving luggage, and so on. SIA has tried to be the best in both aspects of product and service innovation, and has won numerous awards as a result.

The core values of the airline are:

- pursuit of excellence
- safety
- customer priority
- concern for staff
- integrity
- teamwork

Nothing really spectacular about SIA's core values that would differentiate it from many others in many industries, but as we know, it is how the brand experience is managed that can create an outstanding image, and this is what SIA has done well.

It has managed the service issue through the creation of service value attributes, which are:

- caring—being helpful, sensitive to passengers' needs, patient, tactful, hospitable

- warm—being pleasant, courteous, cheerful
- professional—being knowledgeable, skillful, confident, efficient, well-groomed
- enterprising—being adaptable, proactive, resourceful, responsive, spontaneous, using initiative
- dedicated: being committed, conscientious

Brand personality

SIA's service values are really its brand personality, the application of which, through the personification of the "Singapore Girl," has delivered the brand image. Created in 1973, the Singapore Girl was the software of the business, with in-flight crew dressed in attractive Pierre Balmain designed Malay *Sarong Kebaya*. A youth policy was imposed on cabin crew, and substantial training given to insure a consistent personality, even down to company dental check-ups and personal grooming rules. The advertising support for many years was well executed, and the Singapore Girl became an icon.

Brand positioning

In positioning terms, SIA did well on both dimensions of importance to the consumer—technology and service—compared to other airlines. However, the perceptual gap has narrowed in the last few years. While continuing to be seen as an airline with a young and modern fleet, recent research reveals that SIA has lost some ground on the service dimension, which is not as good as it used to be compared to other airlines. It appears to have lost some of the consistency it once had.

Brand management

The task for SIA now is to balance its expansion with the customer experience. It must continue to pursue the innovative record it has and work hard to regain ground on the service aspects. This issue is currently being addressed through a large-scale human-resource initiative called Transforming Customer Service (TCS), which focuses on all staff in the service chain. Dr Cheong says: "We are talking about adopting a whole new mindset towards our customers. We are talking about empowering frontline service staff to seize service opportunities as they arise." The TCS program is about turning customers into SIA ambassadors, and will operate at all levels of the organization.

At the individual level, frontline staff will be able to deliver a more personalized and innovative service through a flexible approach at corporate level to systems and procedures.

Advertising execution also appears to be in need of improvement, in image as opposed to product terms. While consistency remains, new and refreshing ways of delivering the same key messages seem to be somewhat lacking.

There is also the issue of airline alliances, designed to provide consumers with ease of travel wherever they want to go by dealing with one airline. This brings with it for SIA the problem that most other airlines have now, which is providing the customers with a seamless brand experience when the image of one airline depends to some extent on the experience of traveling with their airline partners.

Brand strengths: innovation, focus on customer experience, consistency of brand messages, continual high level of brand investment, even in recession.

Case Study 2

BANYAN TREE HOTELS & RESORTS
A role model for brand
guardianship in a niche-market

From product to brand

Banyan Tree Hotels & Resorts started as a niche product—it was thought of as a product and was managed as such. It was designed as a range of small and exclusive high quality villa hotels offering seclusion. Features, attributes, quality of service, customer benefits, and product delivery were uppermost in the minds of management. Its success is legendary.

This is not to say that its initial success was accidental—far from it. There was a gap in the market that the top-class giant hotels, such as the Sheraton and Shangri-La groups could not provide. There was a niche-market position that could be seized and owned, and one where competition was limited. The idea was that there existed a market segment composed of people who wanted to stay in accommodation that offered privacy, seclusion, and luxury in a special and intimate way.

The success was so immediate and intense that the company expanded rapidly. It did so both with its own product and, because of its reputation and its proven track record, by taking up offers from other property groups which have outsourced the management of their businesses in a bid to improve their standards. This meant on occasion giving away the Banyan Tree name along with the management expertise. But, these joint ventures did not reach the standards of the original product. The growth of the company and the extension of its brand in this way could have been disastrous for the Banyan Tree image, but the astute early realization that the product had become a brand led to the rapid recovery of brand control.

Business growth versus brand guardianship

The protection of the brand is now a top priority for the company. It has made a definitive decision to forego many other contract-management opportunities, which could have been extremely lucrative, so that the Banyan Tree brand equity that had been built up will not become diluted. The temptation to go for short-term profits and revenue enhancement has been rejected in favor of building long-term, and somewhat intangible, brand value.

Brand extension

What the company has now done, in the way of extending the brand, is to launch the Banyan Tree Spa, which is absolutely consistent and appropriate to the core of the brand. From the tag line, "Sanctuary for the Senses," to product, everything is magnificent, and the product description seems to embody the brand mission when it says the spa is:

"A sanctuary for the body and mind, offering personal rejuvenation. Combining caring and friendly staff with an ambience of solitude, luxury, and peace, where the outside world is almost forgotten."

The spa offers massotherapy, body treatment, hydrotherapy, special nutrition, and many health packages, with names like Sea of Senses, Oasis of Harmony, and Voyage of Peace.

Brand attributes to brand personality

The brand personality of Banyan Tree has evolved as a result of this process. While many of the original characteristics, such as being small, professional, quality-oriented, exclusive, confident, sophisticated, and others, were and still are relevant and important, the two personality characteristics that are now predominant and consistently reinforced are:

- romance
- intimacy

These have become the true positioning of Banyan Tree Hotels & Resorts, and are the focus of the customer brand experience.

The brand experience

Needless to say, the brand fulfills its promise and delivers the romance and intimacy of its character. Almost each villa is secluded with its own pool, open terraces with fabulous views, four-poster bed, a seductive atmosphere, and other appropriate facilities. The lucky couple (for the market-segment focus is on couples) will literally be cocooned in luxury. Everything is sensual and romantic, inviting those intimate moments. It is meant to give people the fantasy they have always dreamed of but thought they could never achieve. As for marketing communications, all advertisements and collaterals are also consistent with, and appropriate to, the brand personality and experience. Banyan Tree Hotels & Resorts has won many international awards, most notably for its ongoing efforts in conserving the environment.

Brand building at speed

Many companies believe that brand building takes decades, and in many categories it does, especially if it competes at the mass-consumer level. But, this is not necessarily so in niche-markets. In a recent survey of Asian brands (excluding Japanese), Banyan Tree Hotels & Resorts ranked 18, and it is less than four years old. This does not reflect the company's strategic view of building a brand, where long-term investment is seen as essential. What it does reflect is the ability to spot a niche-market, develop a unique product and brand personality to meet that market's needs, and an absolute obsession with brand guardianship.

International to global?

Banyan Tree Hotels & Resorts is already an international brand, and there is no doubt that it can become a global brand, but has it got global ambitions? Chairman Ho Kwon Ping says the company would like a world presence, but this will be approached with caution. It would very much like a presence in the Caribbean, the Seychelles, and other exotic destinations, but sensibly is consolidating its regional leadership position, and only taking further steps that are controllable from a total brand perspective. The brand is everything—an entity to be nurtured, protected, and allowed to grow in a controlled and consistent fashion.

Brand strengths: niche-market positioning and differentiation, outstanding quality product, unique personality backed by the brand experience, consistent, appropriate marketing communications, obsessive brand guardianship.

WHEREVER THERE'S A BANYAN TREE,

ROMANCE WILL BLOSSOM.

(Reproduced with permission from Banyan Tree Hotels & Resorts)

Advertisement featuring the unique brand personality of
Banyan Tree Hotels & Resorts.

Case Study 3

GUCCI
Revitalizing an old brand

In 1993, Gucci, now one of the world's most famous brands, lost US$22 million on revenues of US$230 million. It was then known for matronly women's wear, and had no ready-to-wear lines. It was taken over by Investcorp, and family control passed out of the Gucci family's hands. Domenico de Sole was kept on to manage the business, and Thomas Ford promoted to the job of head designer. To turn the business around, a total change was necessary. But, the key to the revitalization was Domenico's insistence that Gucci was not a retailer but a brand, and there are evidently occasions when he would get quite angry with people who chose to differ.

The product lines were changed to add color and ready-to-wear items, and Gucci held ready-to-wear shows. People liked the retro 1960s designs by Ford, and by 1995, a profit of US$8.5 million was made on revenues of US$500 million.

Traditionally, distribution had been in the hands of three different types of entities, namely,

- stores operated directly by Gucci
- franchised stores
- department store boutiques and duty-free shops

Gucci spent over US$200 million buying back franchises, opened new directly operated stores, and refurbished the old ones with a new look. This gave it the control and consistency necessary to make a great brand. The rest is history, and Gucci is now one of the most respected brands in the world, and the subject of ambitious takeover plans.

Brand strengths: prestige and aspirational positioning, brand-management revival, brand name.

6

Measuring Brand Success

THE USE OF MARKET RESEARCH

Quantitative and qualitative research

Over the last two decades, the tremendous growth in purchasing power in most Asian countries, coupled with the vast choices of brands available, have led purchase decisions away from price sensitivity and more towards brand association and positioning factors. This has led to a huge growth in the market research industry as more companies try to understand consumer motivations. Market research tends to be executed on the quantitative side, but less so on the qualitative side. Western research companies have opened up many Asian operations, and formed many partnerships with Asian companies, just as branded goods companies have, and the full range of research services is improving fast.

Both quantitative and qualitative research methods are used to study brand success, sometimes separately and sometimes together. Good qualitative research is essential in understanding brand success. Although the two research methods overlap to a certain extent, there is a basic difference between them.

Quantitative research essentially shows what is happening. It can tell, for example, the size of a market for a particular brand category and the different brand shares, who buys what and at what price, where and how these customers can be reached, and other such information. It often involves the use of scaled questionnaires to assess the degree of brand awareness and the strength of people's preferences for different brand attributes. As a result, it is often used to track over time what consumers know about brands relative to the competition.

Qualitative research essentially explains why something is happening. It will show, for example, why people like a brand and the associations they have with it, what they expect from it and how they relate to its personality and values, relative to other brands. This type of research relies more on face-to-face discussions and activities such as focus groups, and less on heavily structured methodology.

In order to be successful at branding, two factors have to be developed when trying to build a relationship between a brand and its audience:

• brand awareness
• brand association

Together, quantitative and qualitative research can provide information that will help companies a great deal towards understanding consumer behavior, particularly on brand awareness and brand association, and it is these two aspects that need to be understood for brand-strategy purposes.

Brand awareness

Creating brand awareness is a prerequisite for building a relationship. In a sense, it is the "getting-to-know-you" phase. There is an obvious link between awareness and purchase because people will not buy something they do not know anything about. However, in branding, awareness is more than this initial phase of a relationship because people will first have to relate the brand itself (its identity or personality) to its category, and the range of uses it may possess.

Brand awareness involves brand recognition and brand recall. Brand recognition involves people simply being able to recognize the brand as being different from others by seeing it or hearing it after they have already been acquainted with it. Logos, slogans, names, and packaging— visual identity items in general—facilitate this. They are particularly important for fast-moving consumer goods at the point of purchase because people often buy the brand after noticing it is there and realizing they need something from that category. Brand recall is a term used to describe how well people can remember the brand when they are prompted by the name of the category or the usage situation. This is important when consumers plan category purchases in advance. Both of these concepts are easily researchable, and are often used by companies after brand launches and stimulatory campaigns, and on a regular-tracking basis.

Brand associations

To really stand out from the crowd, a brand has to have a relationship with the consumer. Brands succeed when they establish not just a rational relationship, but also an emotional association that people feel strongly about. Once the logic of buying a product or a service is established, it is the emotional attachment that makes the difference. There are opportunities, even in commodity-type markets, to reach out to the consumer if only their feelings about the items they buy are understood. The following is an example of how even unexciting commodity products can have the opportunity to be turned into brands that have unique emotional associations.

How does a brand make you feel?

In the U.K., which has a population of around 58 million, it is estimated that £1.8 billion is spent annually on household detergents and cleaning products (e.g. soap, powder, or bleach). The market is crowded and supermarket shelves are packed with product choices with various features and attributes. A recent research with focus groups of housewives—those principally involved in purchasing these items, and often doing the cleaning—revealed several interesting facts.

- Housewives were found to actually loathe shopping for these products. The shopping experience was deemed to be uninteresting and dull.
- When asked with what they associated household cleaning, the housewives answered with phrases such as
  - coffee marks on tables
  - stubborn stains on furniture and carpets

- ◆ messes children, especially babies, make everywhere
- ◆ hairs from family pets
- ◆ other unpalatable thoughts
- When housewives were asked how they felt about having to actually do the household cleaning, most of the words used in their replies were strongly negative, and included "hate" and "delaying me from doing other things."
- Further, the housewives felt that the packaging of cleaning products was ugly, full of jargon and industrial language, and sometimes downright unintelligible.
- When filmed shopping for these products in supermarkets, women were seen to be dithering in the aisles wondering which brand to buy, with unhappy expressions on their faces.
- However, the really interesting fact found was that when housewives were asked what household cleaning was all about, they gave replies such as caring for the health of the family. Also, since they were going to have to do it, they would like it to be more fun, with products that fitted their lifestyles and preferences. So, they suggested product innovations such as
  - ◆ different smells for different rooms, e.g. pine for the bathroom, lemon for the kitchen
  - ◆ different colors, e.g. lilac, mauve
  - ◆ visuals and smells of flowers and fruits

The problem in the U.K. is that cleaning products were presented in the same way; the situation is the same in Asia. The brands are designed to appeal to the rational part of people's minds. There is no emotion attached to the brands, no nice visual in packaging, and no appeal to the emotional part of women's lives. All that the manufacturers were doing was making an unpleasant experience more so. The balance is wrong. In categories like this, emotion is important, because housewives feel emotional about what the products are and do. They do not want technology and science, do not care about "concentrated" or "non-concentrated," "biological," or "non-biological." Cleaners are expected to clean things, so attributes of the rational kind do not offer the differentiation, nor do features and attributes have a great influence on what brand is bought. Generating a brand that stands out from the crowd will take liberal doses of emotion because surveys have shown that the target audience feels emotional about the product experience.

The opportunity is there for innovation, lifestyle, and emotional branding. Understanding consumers' thoughts is vital, and the emotional and rational balance is necessary to create an outstanding brand. It might not be too long before we see designer detergents.

This is a good example of how qualitative research can discover the hidden feelings and associations consumers have with brands and categories of brands. This type of research can lead to a whole new way of looking at the market, and in this case, might lead to the development of a new brand category.

Brand personality

There are many qualitative research techniques that can reveal how people think and feel about a brand in terms of its personality. These techniques include:

- obituary writing—getting brand users to write about the brand as though it was recently deceased
- what ifs—describing a brand if it was, say, a car, a room, a holiday destination, or an animal, and comparing the answers to those of other brands
- brand talk—using matchstick and bubble drawings to get consumers to fill in what a brand would say to other brands, and vice versa
- collages—e.g. using photographs to allow consumers to develop a picture of what a brand looks like compared to other brands

These exercises can be both revealing and fun to carry out, and can be tried out with the company staff too.

More elaborate tracking studies can be used to continually evaluate a brand's performance against the competition on its chosen values or personality characteristics. These are best done on a regular basis as occasional "dipstick" measurements may not be too accurate nor show trends or how consumer perceptions are influenced by various campaigns.

Perceptual mapping for brand tracking and strategy

Brand image is a summary of consumer perceptions. Research techniques are available that can produce visual representations of how consumers see brands as being similar or different on various dimensions. Judicious use of several techniques can present reflections of consumers' minds, allowing us to judge the positions that several brands occupy relative to each other in consumers' minds. These reflections are called perceptual maps, and are usually, though not always, two-dimensional.

In the following case study on beer in Thailand, perceptual mapping was used to look at strategic brand-positioning options and new product opportunities. Boon Rawd Brewery also shows how the judicious use of qualitative and quantitative research methods can help diagnose a competitive issue and provide information for strategic positioning purposes.

Case Study 1

BOON RAWD BREWERY
Researching beer brand image
and strategy options in Thailand

This case study brings together quantitative and qualitative research methods to produce some powerful insights into consumer preferences and associations, and reveals alternative brand-positioning strategies. Boon Rawd Brewery is a household name in Thailand, and has an exemplary image as a good employer and well-managed company with a strong record of social responsibility. The most famous of the company's products is Singha beer.

A research study, initiated by the company, was designed to elicit the positions of certain brands of beer in the minds of consumers, and the associations that were most important to the consumers. The study was also designed to reveal strategic opportunities for new and existing products. The research team brought together a series of customers in several focus groups, in the key geographic markets of Bangkok and Chiangmai.

Participants were first asked to fill in a short questionnaire on the attributes they thought were important in choosing a brand.

Participants were then asked to consider the six brands of beer predominant in the Thailand beer market. These were:

- Heineken, a global premium brand, originating from Holland, and has seen good growth in market share in previous years
- Carlsberg, another global brand and originating from Denmark
- Singha, the traditional Thai beer, which had undergone some image development in previous years to increase its acceptability with younger, affluent groups
- Kloster, a beer made in Thailand, but branded and positioned as a European beer
- Leo, a lower-priced beer that was marketed primarily on a low price—lower quality strategy
- Chang, a recent entrant, brought in on a low-cost strategy to take the lower-end rural market

Participants were then asked to rate how similar they thought these brands were with each other. As customers were not asked specific questions about the brands, they were allowed to compare the brands on their own set of criteria. As is the case with most perceptions of brand image, they are often unconsciously made and sometimes difficult to describe verbally. This rating process meant that the researchers' preconceived assumptions about the importance of brand attributes like taste, color, and the even more important personality characteristics such as prestige, softness or hardness, friendliness, and so on, did not interfere with developing these image maps.

How closely each person and each group of people thought the six brands were related, can be summarized in a chart, produced using a technique called multi-dimensional scaling.

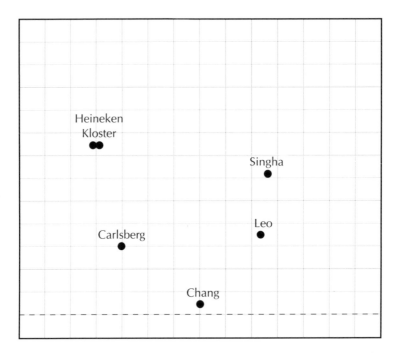

Figure 10: Market perception of six beer brands in Thailand.

Figure 10 shows a perceptual map. Each dimension on the graph can be interpreted as an attribute that causes the consumers to differentiate between the products. At this stage of the research, the dimensions (axes) were unknown, but the relative distances between the brands are a direct mathematical representation of the "product space" as perceived by the consumer.

It can be seen clearly that Heineken and Kloster were perceived as being very similar to each other, but different from Singha, Carlsberg, Leo, and Chang. However, it can also be seen that Heineken, Kloster, and Carlsberg were similarly perceived on the horizontal dimension, when compared to Singha and Leo, with Chang being positioned in the middle. On the vertical dimension, there is less differentiation, but it can be seen that Heineken and Kloster, followed closely by Singha, were positioned at one end of the dimension, with Chang at the other end.

Interpreting these dimensions is key to developing a strategy, and the preciseness with which the dimensions can be defined has a major impact on the validity of the final strategies. This would have to be done next.

Interpretation is a subjective process that, nevertheless, includes the assistance of some statistical methods. If a researcher knows beforehand some of the attributes that are important to a certain market, these attributes can be presented directly to consumers, and brands can again be compared based on these attributes. Several attributes such as cost, taste, image, and packaging were tested, and then overlaid on the map that had been generated.

Interestingly, the cost dimension did not seem to be highly related to brand choices in this sample of fairly affluent, moderate to heavy beer drinkers. However, some image attributes were highly related, though any one attribute could not explain the difference in the positions completely.

The transcripts and observations from the focus groups also helped in the interpretation. These subjective perceptions of the brands included dimensions that the researchers could not have possibly anticipated, and several perceptions took the researchers by surprise.

For example, when asked what Singha would look like if the beer were a person (i.e. Mr Singha), almost all groups of participants mentioned words and phrases such as friendly, casual, easy to get to know, joker, casually dressed, local, and good-hearted. Mr Heineken was seen as sober, serious, successful, a little aloof, wearing a smart suit with accessories, and European.

Participants also were asked to imagine situations in which they would consume the different brands. In social situations, for example, many said they would consume the more prestigious and expensive brands, but at home they would consume the cheaper ones like Leo and Chang. In describing the Singha brand, many recalled with smiling faces, happy situations involving family, friends, and natural settings such as sitting by a river and fishing. In describing the Heineken brand, they recalled business and more serious situations or formal occasions such as weddings, company social functions, or situations where they wanted to make a good impression.

All of this data helped interpret the dimensions on the perceptual map.

Further information helped in describing the brand images. For example, before the focus groups were held, several lifestyle images were developed based on previous in-company research, general lifestyle research of Thai consumers, and images used in the international beer industry. These images described the sort of lifestyle that consumers may aspire to, elements of which could be built into the final product through product design, packaging, and promotion. These were refined and eventually defined:

- the Master European Brewer—a personality based on that of existing beer brands which are marketed on the competence of their makers, professionalism, craftsmanship, and their origin in countries renowned for the art of brewing
- the International Thai—essentially, reflects the Thai who is proud of Thailand's positive attributes; is proud of being Thai, yet is a citizen of the world and knows the difference between jingoism and genuine attributes of Thailand as seen from abroad; modern and ambitious—wants to achieve success internationally
- the Modern Thai—a rough Thai equivalent of the yuppie and has strong similarities to this group around the world; young, fashion-conscious, professional, and well-educated achiever who looks to status symbols and wishes to set himself or herself apart from those who have not achieved as much; in contrast to the International Thai who seeks respect internationally, the Modern Thai seeks respect locally and usually has a strong local network; has high disposable income and invests some of it in symbols of achievement like consuming premium or quality beer, a

well-known trait; also has some characteristics in common with the International Thai, but is more of a local person with not as great an aspiration as the International Thai to achieve internationally or share similar interest in Thailand's place in the world

- the Cosmopolitan World Traveler—a confident, adventurous, successful, and culturally-aware individual; more "international" than any of the other personalities and has little relation directly to "Thai-ness" or specific Thai values as do the Modern and International Thai; but like the International Thai, is international in outlook; cares less about Thailand's role in the world unlike the International Thai

- the Heritage Thai—a personality that appeals to those who value heritage, and in Thailand this includes Thai heritage in particular; a more mature personality, is reliable and respects values and traditions like family; Boon Rawd's corporate image and many of its advertisements reflect this personality.

Towards the end of each focus group, participants were asked to comment on these images as well as describe how they fitted with the images of existing products. Each image was accompanied by a summary, which included the key words and phrases associated with that image.

Just as the previously known attributes were superimposed onto the perceptual map, so too were trial personalities or images by asking the participants to again rate each brand against each of these five images.

Although there were some important differences between groups in relation to their geographic location, sex, age, nominated favorite brand, and frequency of product usage, some perceptions seemed to be uniform throughout the group. These general perceptions are usually the most valid and salient, especially with a broad-based campaign such as the ones used in beer advertising.

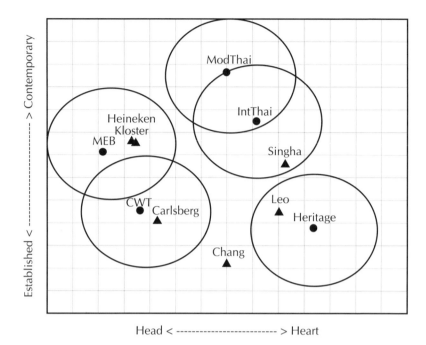

Figure 11: Superimposing brand and brand personalities.

Figure 11 shows the positions of these five "virtual images" on the perceptual map. Note how Heineken and Kloster represent well the Master European Brewer "space", while Carlsberg appears slightly off-center in the Cosmopolitan World Traveler space. Singha appears on the edge of the International Thai space while Leo represents the Heritage Thai dimension. Chang does not seem to be able to represent any of the images. As a low-priced brand and the cheapest on the market, sold in bulk with a whisky product via a predominantly rural market, Chang seemed to compete mainly on price. As several focus group participants mentioned: "You drink Chang to get drunk!" The Modern Thai space does not appear to be served by any product.

The next step was to finally interpret the dimensions. After analyzing the contents of the focus group transcripts and using the previous attributes and the virtual images as a guide, it was possible to label the vertical dimension as Established–

Contemporary and the horizontal dimension as Heart–Head.

The brands towards the top of the Established–Contemporary dimension had a more modern, new, up-to-date, fresh, and present or future image, as compared to the brands towards the bottom, which were perceived as traditional, established, and consumed by older and more conservative people.

The brands towards the left of the Head–Heart dimension were perceived as more logical and serious, while those towards the right were perceived as appealing more to the heart.

Having drawn out the map for these five major images and the six brands, the strategies could now be formulated

First of all, the global brands were clustered towards the Head dimension, although local brand Kloster was also perceived similarly—Kloster's marketers had given it a European image by using a European name. Interestingly, Kloster's previous tag line was "Happiness you can drink," a clever line that would have appealed to the Thai sense of informality and fun, but nowadays the brand is more associated with the more sober Head image and has lost market share over time.

Brand strategy and re-positioning options

Several strategies are available to Boon Rawd to differentiate its brands from those of its competitors and to compete effectively as shown in Figure 12. The arrows represent possible directions for re-positioning existing brands. The large dots represent possibilities for the introduction of new products.

The options for Boon Rawd are to create a Master-European-Brewer brand itself and compete in the market place, directly against the global brands and Kloster. Kloster had demonstrated that even though it is a local brand, it could create an image as an international brand. However, there are some hidden traps with this approach. Several focus-group participants mentioned that they thought Kloster lost some credibility by

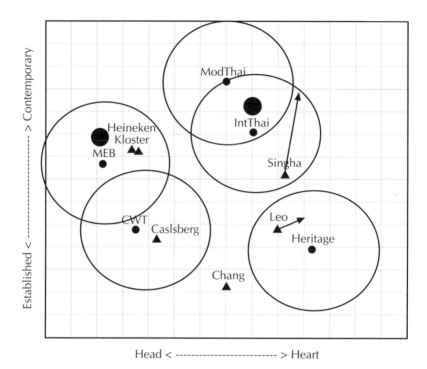

Head < ------------------------- > Heart

Figure 12: Brand strategy and re-positioning options.

being a local brand dressed up in international clothing (the issue of country of origin). Furthermore, the Master European Brewer space, though obviously a valuable one (whether it will grow faster or slower in the immediate future is dependent on the rate of Thailand's economic recovery), is already crowded.

Another strategy to regain some of the market share that Singha had lost due to the entry of the global brands and low-end products, was to re-position the Singha product itself. It was sensed that Singha possessed a great deal of customer loyalty and one strategy would be to develop Singha to be even more Heart-based, and to move further into the International Thai space. This could be accomplished by an integrated marketing communications campaign.

A further option would be to develop a Singha-export brand and prove that Singha could be accepted worldwide. This would appeal particularly to those who identify with the International Thai image. Should Singa be accepted internationally, it would instill pride in Thai consumers in that they are consuming a Thai product that is recognized internationally, targeting in a tangential but strategic way, the monopoly global brands have on internationalism.

For reasons of confidentiality, further information is not available, but the study has been of immense use to strategic thinking.

Central to the above case study is the interaction of quantitative and qualitative methodology in creating a brand strategy. Qualitative techniques can provide richness of data, necessary for delving into the often unconscious brand images that customers may already have of a product, thus allowing companies to build on them. Quantitative techniques can provide objective evidence about subjective assumptions that have a basis in reality. Both research techniques are required for successful brand-image and positioning-strategy research. Finally, it should be mentioned that market research is only a guide to strategic thinking, and does not present complete solutions for brand strategy. It does, however, help paint in the full picture, especially with respect to consumer thinking.

Source: Orient Pacific Century (www.orientpacific.com)

7

Developing International
Asian Brands —
Problems and Opportunities

Asia faces a bleak future should building local brands become the norm. Asian companies must develop international and global aspirations, although they might be forgiven for wondering if it is at all possible to build an international or even a global brand now, given that many markets are already dominated by major brands that have established themselves over many decades. Despite this, there are still many opportunities for Asian companies to do so, especially since world markets are changing so fast. However, there are certain fundamental prerequisites that need to be put in place before any brand can attempt to achieve international or global status.

GLOBAL AND INTERNATIONAL BRANDS

True global brands are relatively few in number. What is a global brand, and how does a global brand differ from an international brand? Most people would reply, if asked, that a global brand is one that has world market coverage, and to a certain extent the reply would be right. Taking Coca-Cola and McDonald's as two prime examples, there are few countries in the world that these two brands have yet to enter. So in a sense, a global brand is one that is present in most markets in the world.

There are, on the other hand, some international players with globally known brands that are not global in coverage, either because the company has chosen to avoid that route or because the product is

175

not acceptable the world over. Marks & Spencer is a world famous company with its St Michael brand, but it has chosen not to attempt to develop a truly global presence.

A differentiating factor between some global and international brands might be that global brands keep the same name whichever country they are in. Some companies that are involved in as many markets do not do this. For example, British American Tobacco does not have a cigarette brand that keeps its name whatever market it is in, but Philip Morris's Marlboro does. Names are critical to brand success and must be universally acceptable for global branding. Occasionally they have to be translated, but they keep the name as close as possible to the original, or insure a name appropriate to the brand image, as with Coca-Cola in China. Stories are told of names that have or have not been researched well enough, and have proved to be embarrassing failures. One of these was General Motors' world car NOVA that failed in Spain, as the name in the local language literally meant "won't go."

Global brands have universal appeal, not only in their names, but with their product offering as well. In order to satisfy this criterion, they have to be targeted at, and accepted by, global consumer segments. There are many global segments including younger people defined by certain age groupings, young mothers, young professionals, the gray segment of older and retired people, business travelers, and others. The people within each of these segments tend to share similar needs, wants, interests, lifestyles, aspirations, and attitudes. Companies that understand what these are and accordingly develop an idea that leads to an acceptable product, can be successful in creating global brands.

Finally, global brands generally stick to the same basic brand personality, values, and positioning across the world, even though product and communications strategies might be adapted slightly to cater to the nuances of different cultures. The Body Shop, for example, does not alter its position of defending the environment and the creatures in it, despite modifying its product range from country to country. McDonald's is positioned the world over as a family restaurant providing fun and value-for-money meals, but its menu changes with cultural preferences—in Russia, one cannot find the Samurai burger that is offered in some Asian countries.

One major difference between global and international brands then is that global brands offer consumers the same personality and positioning across all markets. They are entirely consistent, whereas international brands that are available globally sometimes position themselves differently or alter their brand personality to suit different audiences. Guinness, for example, is positioned differently around the world depending on its target customer groups. An even tighter definition of global brands would also state that they do not change their product characteristics in any way. This would then include brands like Marlboro but exclude brands like Nescafé that has over one hundred different formulations catering to varied local tastes.

MARKET COVERAGE VERSUS MARKET SHARE

Does it really matter whether a brand is regarded as global or international? Perhaps not. The important thing to consider is how a brand can grow. For instance, one brand can be global in presence but not in terms of market share, while another may have presence in fewer countries around the world but have a high percentage market share in each. It all depends on the appropriate expansion strategy. For example, Airhold NV is regarded as a global retailer with over 3,500 supermarkets in Europe, the Americas, and Asia, but it is present in only 17 countries. Many of Airhold's suppliers are located in over 100 countries. But this does not worry Airhold, which takes the view that to have an impact does not depend on being a global player. To this company, having a decisive share of the markets it is in, is more important.

THE GLOBAL–LOCAL BRANDING DILEMMA

The latest management catchphrase on this issue appears to be: "think glocal" or "think global, act local." But, what do companies have to consider when deciding if and how far they should go towards local brand adaptation? Both global and local branding strategies have their advantages.

Global branding

The main advantages of global branding come with the economies of scale it can provide, particularly in advertising and promotion, public relations, media overlap, packaging, and other marketing activities. In holding fast to a single corporate or product face, design decisions are greatly simplified, as is the case with companies like Shell. Savings generated are likely to be substantial. If the brand is also truly global in terms of product standardization, like Coca-Cola, then there are additional large savings to be made in production, and research and development. Global branding can leverage the resultant global image while still retaining the association of its home country. So, it makes sense for companies to derive as many benefits as they can from global branding. It is not always straightforward though. In big mergers and acquisitions, such as the merger between Mobil and Esso, there may be hundreds of millions of dollars in savings from advertising and promoting just one brand. But, what is the value of the brand equity that would have to be given up by removing one brand name?

Local branding

Companies sometimes find that it is not so easy to impose one brand on the world without taking into account the sensitivities of local markets. Local branding, sometimes referred to as fully adaptive branding, has its benefits too. If a company has decided to embark on this route, it has the freedom to develop brand names, visual elements and associations for each specific audience, and produce them locally. It can also take advantage of the fact that the brand is regarded as a local one.

Global versus local branding decisions

Globally standardized products are more accessible in technology industries. For example, computers and components for electronics products are basically the same the world over, unlike food products that may have to have ingredient changes for certain countries to suit local taste buds. In reality, the choice is not just global versus local branding since a wide range of brand-related activities have to be considered in the global–local decision-making process, including the following:

- brand strategy
  - brand name, logo, slogan, trademark
  - brand personality
  - positioning strategy
  - choice of target-market segments

- marketing activities
  - advertising and promotion
  - distribution channels
  - sales function
  - pricing strategy

- product (service)
  - research and development
  - core features and attributes
  - design
  - packaging

- operations
  - financial management
  - production
  - logistics

When deciding on how to go about developing international brands, the choices will vary between the companies concerned and their products. Companies such as Nestlé and Unilever opt for partial or complete local adaptation on most of these activities. They have, for example, many different names for similar products and ingredient changes for some depending on the country. Companies such as Intel, however, adopt a global stance on many of these issues even though they may manufacture products in many international locations to gain cost advantages.

However the global–local game is played, it is inevitable that any company with a global or international brand will have to accommodate cultural sensitivities. But, there is another major issue that affects Asian companies, and which often causes obstacles to the development of international and global brands: the brand's country of origin.

THE ISSUE OF COUNTRY OF ORIGIN

One of the problems that has dogged Asian companies when trying to build and promote their brands domestically and internationally is the effect of the country of origin on the brand image. In many Asian countries, for example, it is by no means uncommon to hear shoppers exclaim statements such as: "I do not want to buy that brand—it is made here." Similarly, buyers in foreign markets have strong doubts about the quality of Asian products. Traditionally, Asian countries have suffered from "cheap" and "poor quality" images, especially with respect to their manufactured goods. Only Japan has managed to overcome this problem, and it has taken more than two decades to do so, with major brands such as Sony and Canon leading the way. Other Asian countries are still struggling to overcome negative perceptions held by local and foreign consumers. But the fact is Asian production quality is just as good as that of many western countries, according to the big-brand companies. For example, PepsiCo says that its China production facility recently won the Best Quality Award for PepsiCo International. Carlsberg's joint venture in Malaysia won the 1998 World Quality Award for Carlsberg, beating every brew from all countries with local production facilities, including the beer brewed in the home country of Denmark.

So, the reality is that international brands are *perceived* to offer better intrinsic quality than local ones. Two key factors govern the significance of the country of origin to consumers, according to research:

* brand awareness and knowledge
* perceived risk

Country of origin becomes less important as brand familiarity increases and perceived risk decreases.

Brand awareness and knowledge

If products carry a well-known brand name, the issue of country of origin becomes less relevant to the consumer. Consumers are more concerned about origin when products carry an unfamiliar brand name. Research in China by TWBA (Hong Kong) bears this out, with typical comments from Chinese consumers being

"If I am not familiar with certain brands, I will pay attention to its country of origin to be sure of the quality and credibility."
"Brand name comes first. I don't care where Adidas and Coca-Cola come from."

Marketers get mesmerized at the very mention of the China market. Their eyes transform into cash registers and their faces appear dream-like, as they imagine 1.2 billion people rushing to buy their brands. Part of their dream is reality, because brand names in China account for 25–50% of all consumers' intent to make a purchase. At last count, it was estimated that there were up to 100 million yuppies in the country, with big spending power in search of leading brands. Researchers have found that Chinese consumers feel very proud to own international brands that they sometimes leave the maker's tags on their clothes, stickers on sunglasses, etc. However, doing business in China and other Asian countries is not so easy, and companies need to seek advice on how to enter these markets.

Perceived risk

"Made-in" labels have little effect on famous and well-known brand names. The general perception is that well-known brand names deliver on quality no matter where it is made—the brand name gives them re-assurance on authenticity. The perceived risk is, therefore, much reduced.

Because of these factors, companies producing well-known brands are in a better position to take advantage of cheaper production costs and manufacture products in the developing countries.

Country-positioning effect

Some countries occupy distinct positions in the minds of Asian consumers that indicate they have strong associations with certain products and product images. For example, France is associated with luxury consumer items such as cosmetics, clothing, and alcoholic beverages, while the U.S. is associated more with technology and sports products. The Swiss, not surprisingly, are associated with fine prestigious products, the Germans with prestige cars, and Hong Kong with clothing and furniture.

Two factors appear to influence country positioning: price and utility. Western countries (excluding Australia) are perceived as expensive and Asian countries as providing good value. With regards to utility, countries associated strongly with designer and luxury goods are perceived as producing hedonic (pleasure) goods, while those associated with solid build and engineering qualities are perceived as producing more utilitarian or pragmatic products. If there was a chart with the axes representing leisure and pragmatic goods, the U.S. and Japan, which are strongly associated with most products and attributes, would sit towards the middle of the map. France and Italy would be high on the hedonic scale, while Taiwan might be high on the pragmatic scale.

Distancing from country of origin

What can be done to avoid the negative associations of a country of origin which does not favor the product, for example, a prestigious or upmarket brand by a company in a developing country? If the product is to be exported, then one possibility is for the company to set up a production unit in a country that has no negative association with quality, premium products. Second, it would also be advantageous to play down the parent company as much as possible, leaving its name and home country off the packaging altogether. Third, it would be helpful to select a brand name for the product that sounds as though it originates from that part of the world that constitutes the main target audience. Alternatively, it could be a name that sounds as though it originates from a country that has a reputation for that type of product.

The classic example of success with such an approach is Lexus, the car made by Toyota. This product was introduced as a prestige, high quality car, aimed at a western audience in direct competition with other famous brands, particularly BMW. Toyota's image and reputation would not have allowed the new brand to bear the parent company name, as it is associated more with the mass-market cars aimed at lower-income market segments, that is, cars that were not really top-tier quality. Toyota produced the Lexus outside Japan; for example, for the U.S. market, a plant was established there, and it chose a name that was globally acceptable. The Toyota name was not used as an endorsement the way it is used with the other brands in the company's stable, e.g.

Toyota Corolla. This distancing technique proved to be highly successful, and in the U.S. market, Lexus stole a large amount of market share from other brands in the category, including BMW. Had the company decided to market the brand as another line in the Toyota portfolio, consumer perceptions would have worked against its entry into the luxury-car segment, even though the quality was as good, if not better, than some competing brands. Perception can be fact or fiction, but to the people who have a certain perception in their minds, it is reality. In this case, no one would have believed that this manufacturer from Japan could make that quality of vehicle, based on its past knowledge and experience, and Toyota's existing and previous product ranges.

Other Asian brands are also the product of distancing techniques, one of which is Bonia. Italy is the country associated strongly with leather fashion goods and apparel, particularly for men. Bonia is an Italian sounding name, and the brand label is attached to the same types of product, but Bonia is a Malaysian brand. Padini apparel has also been highly successful, again with an Italian sounding name, and again a Malaysian brand. Giordano has had tremendous international success with its Italian name, but it originates from Hong Kong. The mineral water brand, Minere, has a French-sounding name and has French wording on its packaging, but the brand is from Thailand. Vochelle is the brand name of a range of chocolate products made by a Malaysian company that sells all over the world. So, even the choice of brand name can make a big difference to the consumers' perceptions.

Implications for brand building in Asia by foreign companies

The implications of these findings for companies wishing to build brands and market their products in Asia are:

- the country of origin can be a favorable influence on the acceptability of the product; if this is the case, then advertising and promotion should place an emphasis on it and play to the strengths associated with perceptions of the country
- segmentation of target audiences and knowledge about them is important—always carry out research to understand the market

- linking the brand values to the values of the country of origin can be extremely advantageous, e.g. Planet Hollywood, with memorabilia, décor, and menus reminding people of the famous stars of Hollywood movies

- choose appropriate strategic partners, as Pillsbury did when entering the China market (see the case study 1 at the end of this chapter).

Implications for brand building by Asian companies

For Asian companies involved in domestic, regional and international marketing, the implications are:

- to look carefully at the impact the country of origin might have on consumer perceptions, and whether the stereotype image of the country might influence the acceptability of the brand

- that if the product has utilitarian and strong value-for-money associations, then it will be well received domestically and regionally; positioning strategy should reflect this

- that if the product has hedonistic perception, e.g. prestige and fashion goods, then the company will need to consider carefully how it will distance the product from the country of origin, as acceptability could be difficult in all countries; distancing can sometimes be achieved by employing a foreign-sounding brand name, as illustrated in the earlier examples, where a company chose a name that would be associated with a country known for the production of certain product categories

- form good strategic alliances if lacking the resources to go it alone, or seeking to tailor the brand offer to the local market; this is the model favored by Hard Rock Café and Starbucks (see Chapter 9 for the case study on Starbucks)

How can small- and medium-sized businesses take on the giant brands?

This is a question on the minds of many smaller producers of products and services in Asia. The honest answer is that they should not. Why take on the giants when they are already dominating most markets of universal appeal? Instead, they should be concentrating on niche marketing and finding the market segments that have not been served properly. As market fragmentation has already been identified in Chapter 1 as a major market trend, it presents more opportunities for Asian companies to access and defend niche-markets, markets where often the giants cannot or do not want to cater to. Finding a niche is one way of building a brand that can be international or even global in nature.

Niche-market opportunities

When a company finds that many of the major markets are dominated by powerful foreign brands, it is time to remember about market fragmentation. As time goes on, the trend is for markets to split into many sets of customer groups or market segments that want generic products and services tailored to their special preferences. Opportunities, therefore, will arise to serve the needs of customer groups that are not catered to by the giants. Niche-markets are good because they can be profitable. People are often prepared to pay more for a special branded product or service that meets their particular needs, aspirations, or lifestyles. Also, these specialist products or services are relatively easy to defend once the company has broken in and obtained good market share.

Niche-market opportunities arise from market segmentation, the principles and techniques of which are described in Chapter 3. Niche marketing represents one of the great opportunities for Asian businesses. Making specialist products for specialist audiences will be one of the keys to the successful growth of Asian international brands, and there appear to be endless alternatives to explore. Looking at the western brand of Hallmark, the greetings-card producer, gives an indication of this potential. Hallmark is basically in the business of "love" but is constantly searching for new market niches for its products. Traditionally, the greetings-card industry was geared up for celebrations with respect to family and close friends to whom companies like Hallmark could reach out to. Now the company says there are over 1,500 ways of expressing "love" to new segments, like step-families, relatives of relatives, ethnic and religious groups, and even pets. Around

740 creative staff produce 11,000 cards every year for millions of people. So, segmentation principles are indeed important in finding these niches. If one looks hard enough, one will find them.

Concentrate on the service aspect

Asian companies have a particular and unique opportunity to build into the customers' brand experiences the service dimension. The reason for this is that Asian people have personality characteristics that people around the world admire and like. Research carried out on airlines, for example, showed that the service standards experienced have been truly memorable. Singapore Airlines has built its image around service standard excellence, and Malaysia Airlines at its best has received the most outstanding service ratings of any airline.

The generic Asian personality has characteristics of being approachable, warm, polite, kind, tolerant, hospitable, modest, and caring, to highlight a few. These characteristics can help create brand personalities that, if executed well, can outperform many foreign brands, particularly in the service sector. But, they can be applied to any business, because all businesses rely to a great extent on relationships, as does customer experience. As long as these characteristics are defined well, translated into job performance, and held at consistently high standards, the opportunity for developing powerful international brand personalities is clear. Outstanding service certainly helps maintain and even increase brand loyalty.

One issue that must not be forgotten when adding the service dimension, is to insure that when things go wrong—and they always do—service recovery must be fast and complete. This means that companies will have to pay particular attention to the training of staff in this area, because embarrassment and loss of face through feeling responsible for problems is also an Asian trait, and people find it difficult to recover quickly from such things.

After-sales service is also important. The product may be the best, but customers want the reliability and dependability of a good service network. In recent years, this has been one of the brand weaknesses of Asian companies, particularly in the durable and electronics consumer goods categories. Brands from Korea and some other Asian countries have damaged their corporate and product image through lack of a good service network. When choosing distributors in foreign countries, look for service capability as well as sales potential. It is important to get the balance right. Customers expect international brands to have good warranties, convenient service centers, and speedy repair. These are critical for image building through the service dimension.

Branding commodity products

Companies are not always in consumer marketing, and many business-to-business firms wonder how they can build brands like those of their consumer counterparts. They argue that price competition is a more important factor to deal with. Though they do have a point, the principles are the same. For instance, if a company deals in commodity products, segmentation is still important. There are three basic segments of commodity buyers:

- price-only
- price-need
- price-cost

Price-only buyers, who represent up to 50% of the market, are totally price-driven. Nothing will deflect them from their goal of lowest price, unless they have a very good relationship with the salesperson. But single relationships of this kind do not build brands, as business tends to disappear when the salespersons do.

Price-need buyers can differentiate between suppliers on matters other than price although price remains firmly in their minds. The difference between this segment and price-only buyers is that price-need buyers value extra needs or problems they have. For example, they might want technical advice and support, guidance on efficiency usage, after-sales service, convenience of different packaging sizes, special standards of reliability and quality, or other concerns, for which they will be prepared to pay some kind of premium. Their needs will tend to be fairly constant, and it will be important to understand their customer base to find out how to add value. A problem-solving-positioning strategy could be appropriate here.

Then, there are the price-cost buyers, who are concerned about price because it plays its part in their overall cost-reduction plans. This segment consists of people who value things such as speed of service, reliability, and quality, and who might want deviations from the norm to reduce costs, such as storage and transportation assistance, and just-in-time delivery. The benefits of such value-added elements may allow for some premium charges. So, obtaining the big picture of the client's business is important.

Some investigative work clearly has to be done in order to determine the differentiating elements that commodity buyers might want. This necessitates an understanding of their businesses, and those of their customers. Relationships are still important, but it is important only if the relationship is with the brand and not particular staff. It is also important to remember that the rational part of customer behavior plays a more important part in purchase decisions, and added value must support any premium pricing. Again, the brand culture is important, and salespeople must not be allowed to play their own discounting games to get business.

In any market for commodity products, the key is to find as many differentiating factors as possible for the target segments, including technical support, packaging, and other items, and bundling them together into attractive value-added packages. Although this may not receive the price premiums that can be gained with consumer goods, being in a low-cost-low-price environment and volume plus reasonable price premiums can be big business. Companies like DuPont have built their brands this way, becoming renowned for innovation and reliability. Malaysia Mosaics and Sitra Wood provide some good ideas on how smaller businesses can successfully build commodity brands.

There are five case studies in this chapter: Pillsbury illustrates how a foreign company can penetrate local markets; Asian Home Gourmet looks at how a niche product brand has established itself globally; Nautica has sound advice for companies wishing to develop an international brand; Malaysian Mosaics and Sitra Wood show how branding work to great effect in business-to business situations.

Case Study 1

PILLSBURY
Choosing the right partner

Pillsbury, the giant American food company, has penetrated the market in China in a very successful way: by sticking to its core business, but doing it the local way. The company's basic business is putting different types of fillings into dough. Chinese cooking is famous for dumplings which have a variety of different delicious forms such as *pau, tim sum,*and others. Pillsbury made the wise decision not to introduce a new product from abroad and educate the Chinese population to eat it, but to produce well-known Chinese products their way and add value to them. Chinese family recipes from a local partner were used. But for Pillsbury, it was still a matter of putting generous helpings of delicious fillings inside dough. What it added was bright, attractive colorful packaging with, for example, pictures of steaming hot dumplings on the wrapping, the introduction of trays as well as plastic containers to give presentation and convenience choice, and frozen options. Through these innovations, Pillsbury added value in the form of its operational experience and branding skills to a carefully chosen local quality product. A great brand partnership. The result so far has been massive sales, satisfied consumers, and prices twice those of the nearest competitors. This is a good example of a global company giving local markets what they want.

Brand strengths: choosing the right partner, sticking to core business, brand marketing expertise, global and local adaptation.

Case Study 2

ASIAN HOME GOURMET
Small players can position themselves globally

Asian Home Gourmet is a brand created by a Cerebos Pacific Ltd. But, it is the product brand that receives the attention and not the company. The brand product range—spice pastes made from fresh herbs and spices—are high quality convenience products that help consumers prepare different foods in a variety of Asian styles. Potentially, this is a commodity market with a great deal of competition. To survive in Asia, let alone globally, the brand has to somehow convince the consumer that it is different and better. So how does it stand out from the crowd? What can Cerebos Pacific do to convince people to buy its brand, as opposed to the array of competitive sauce additives that are available around the world?

Essentially, the brand has chosen to compete in a niche market. Although there is a substantial market for products of this type, the Asian dimension removes it to a particular category. But, within this still competitive category, the brand strategy will decide whether the brand achieves global presence and status or whether it is perceived only as a commodity. The brand name includes the word "gourmet" that gives it a lift in prestige, but the brand platform created is the key.

The answer lies in an insight used to express Asian values, relative to food, to build the brand personality instead of a traditional approach to positioning Asian foods. Most people love food but for Asian people, the link between food and family values is especially strong. Cooking a meal in Asia is not just an act, but a way of expressing emotion. Like all human beings, Asian people are emotional, but it is not the Asian way to outwardly express these emotions. They are, therefore, somewhat repressed. There is also a tremendous respect for the family as an institution, a value that appears to be, if not on the decline, and is certainly less strong in the

West. So when Asians cook meals for their families, it is more an expression of love as opposed to a chore. When they cook for friends, it is a gesture of respect and happiness for that friendship. When they cook for someone they love, it is an ingredient of romance. Food has special status in Asia. As Guy Murphy, strategic planning director of Bartle, Bogle and Hegarty (BBH), the advertising agency for Asian Home Gourmet says: "In Asia, food is a proxy for showing emotion. While people the world over have an emotional relationship with food, that relationship appears to be most intense in the Asian region."

BBH Asia-Pacific devised a campaign that brought together the brand personality and Asian values, and superbly called though not surprisingly, "Recipes made with love." The television commercials, for example, animate ingredients like chillies that intertwine with affection and a family of herbs holding hands. Print advertisements are portrayed visually with a modern but tastefully designed cookbook design. The main ingredients express the emotion on the left-hand page and the words are on the right side.

The product description is: "Our spice pastes are made from fresh herbs and spices. You can use them to create any one of a range of authentic Asian dishes. All you have to add is one important ingredient. A little of yourself."

This is a wonderful example of how an Asian brand can project itself by projecting a personality based on values from the region of origin, together with a positioning that combines a combination of strategies, including emotion. After initially being available only in Asia, it has gone global in its chosen niche market, using emotional values that have universal appeal.

Brand strengths: personality; a combination of features and attributes; rational, emotional and aspirational positioning strategies; excellent use of animation in communicating brand values.

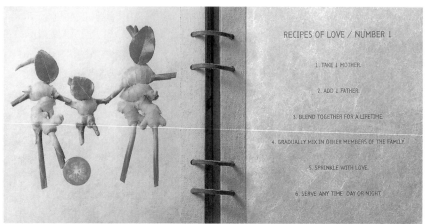

RECIPES OF LOVE / NUMBER 1

1. TAKE 1 MOTHER.

2. ADD 1 FATHER.

3. BLEND TOGETHER FOR A LIFETIME.

4. GRADUALLY MIX IN OTHER MEMBERS OF THE FAMILY.

5. SPRINKLE WITH LOVE.

6. SERVE ANY TIME DAY OR NIGHT.

(Reproduced with permission from BBH Asia-Pacific).

Poster advertisment of Asian Home Gourmet

Case Study 3

NAUTICA
What makes an international brand?

Taiwanese-born David Chu started Nautica, a fashion clothing, accessories, and lifestyle products empire, in 1983 with just six men's designs. Nautica's products are now marketed around the world in over 40 countries. In an interview on CNBC Asia's television program *Managing Asia*, the founder and CEO explained his philosophy of what makes an international brand.

Chu stressed that a quality product is absolutely essential. Products have to perform, and to become an international brand, product quality has to be outstanding and totally consistent. This is particularly important because consumers are very risk-averse and need to have complete trust in the brand they prefer.

A second requirement, according to Chu, is product innovation. This is more obvious in the fashion world where innovation is the norm. But it is also true for any other industry and market. Fashion needs to be progressive, says Chu, but creativity has to be controlled. Companies have to get a good balance and carefully consider what is acceptable to their customers. A big dilemma facing fashion brands is how to constantly innovate in order to keep up with and set fashion trends, and yet still give loyal customers the classic brand style, identity, and value that they have come to expect. Even world-famous brands must be careful with product innovation and not overstep the mark, as Coca-Cola did in its famous relaunch subsequently named Black Friday. The need to balance creativity and innovation with discipline is paramount.

Chu also confirms that to make it internationally, brands need to have ideas and names that enjoy universal appeal. They must stand out, be desirable, and have a specific positioning for a specific target audience. Nautica's product positioning is related to value for money, and it knows who its customers are. It is not *haute couture* or mass market, but is aimed at those people who have an active lifestyle and use active sportswear. In Chu's words, "you must know what you want and be focused." However, despite compounded growth of 35% over the last 15 years, mistakes have been made, for example in brand extension to women's wear in 1996, which did not perform to expectations. It is not easy to fit a total concept embracing function, fashion, and lifestyle to all market segments with instant success, although the company has now also ventured into children's and household items.

Another problem faced by companies trying to develop international brands is the need to control the consistency of quality, delivery, advertising, and other important elements. This can prove to be very difficult, as expansion often requires strategic alliances, such as sub-contracting of production international licensing operations, and similar arrangements. Nautica has resolved many of these potential problems by

- choosing its partners carefully and developing close working relationships with them
- putting its design teams to work with its partners

- overseeing distribution
- monitoring quality
- controling advertising and promotion to achieve consistency in messages and controlling its image around the world.

This is wise brand guardianship, and is vital to success. Companies that sustain their competitive advantage and brand leadership always demonstrate this commitment without compromise. Chu says this is the hardest challenge of all—to achieve consistency and cohesion between brand and concept. What else makes a great brand? The founder of Nautica insists that the forcing of quality, innovation and lifestyle relationships into one place is critical for companies like his.

Chu's final words of advice for those wanting to build a global or international brand are: "You must have a vision and a passion for your product." Most of the giant brands owe their position today to the global visions and passion of their founders. Disney and Gillette are prime examples. With an ambition to move Nautica from international to global brand status in the next few years, and a noticeable passion for his business, Chu looks set to achieve his goals.

Brand strengths: quality, innovation, well-chosen strategic alliances and partnerships, overall brand consistency through brand guardianship, passion.

Case Study 4

MALAYSIAN MOSAICS
Business-to-business global branding

When people think about world-class quality ceramic tiles of beauty, style, and grace, they might be forgiven for thinking of Italy and other European countries. But Asia has its own internationally renown brand. Malaysian Mosaics Berhad has stolen a lot of glory and market share from the world's top producers, and is now positioned clearly as an international player with its MML brand. From Malaysia's new Kuala Lumpur International Airport to Citibank in Vietnam, from Singapore's Mandarin Hotel to Sydney's 2000 Olympic Stadium, you will find its products.

Malaysia's first manufacturer of industrial and homogenous tiles has been operating for 35 years and has an outstanding passion and reputation for quality. It has achieved ISO 9002 standard and has tested and conformed to numerous other quality standards around the world. Its latest fifth generation of porcelain granite tiles were introduced in July 1998 and look like natural stone in appearance—it contains the same materials as natural stones but are produced by a computerized manufacturing process that is state of the art in the industry. They are produced at a futuristic-looking plant, which has an output of 12,000 square meters of tiles per day. Even the Italians acknowledge that this is one of the most technologically advanced tile factories in the world today.

But how has Malaysian Mosaics managed to penetrate international markets from an Asian base, Western perceptions of which some are those of dubious quality—the typical country-of-origin problem discussed earlier—and how has it transformed a business-to-business product into a sought-after brand? The answer lies in a combination of unrivaled quality and service.

Perceptions

The industry's premium segment was traditionally dominated by top-class granite and marble products. The MML-branded, man-made natural product, (containing many of the same elements found in those stones), has a greater strength factor of three times that of granite and a lower price. This meant that changing perceptions was a major issue. The company spent a great deal of time working with trade personnel to convince them that world-class products could be produced at competitive prices. The positioning was price-quality-based, but the MML brand entered a premium segment product, therefore, perceptions had to be steadily managed to accommodate this apparent paradox. The perception gap has still not been completely closed, but this is a strong company goal.

Quality

The search for the best quality has never ceased—in fact the brand mission is: To have the highest quality in its category in the world—and has involved buying the best equipment and expertise from all parts of the world. There was a conscious decision not to spend vast amounts of money on advertising and promotion, but instead to concentrate on thoroughly researching the target countries. The company worked closely with architects, contractors, distributors, and other opinion formers and influencers, using focus groups both to elicit fashion and lifestyle trends, gain information on desired quality levels, and to educate these groups about their products. The main way in which perceptions were changed was to convince these groups of people to try the product to prove the unbelievable claims.

This strategy is reminiscent of the route taken by the Japanese many years ago, when they had to overcome strong prejudice in terms of quality and price. Quality control is taken extremely seriously, and there are random checks on 10% of all final products. If any defects are found in any samples, the entire batch is subjected to checks. The man-made porcelain granite tiles are impervious to acids, pollutants, and frost, have unadulterated color, and are easy to maintain and clean.

Distribution

This is always a critical factor for exporters, and Malaysian Mosaics paid great attention to the selection of the right partners. The partners helped it with its advertising and promotion investment to gain brand awareness and push the quality message. It also worked with some companies to help them produce their own brands. The distributors were not allowed to sell the products at a lower price than the MML products, however. Contract manufacturing, therefore, was only used as part of a strategy to generate profits to put behind brand building in certain countries, and only for highly reputable distributors. It was a catalyst for building the MML brand, and accounted for no more than a third of profits.

Service

Malaysian Mosaics tries to provide the highest of levels of service. Research teams are assigned to work with distributors, and regular support is given by marketing-team visits. As many distributors operate on Just-In-Time (JIT) inventories, every effort is made to insure these distributors get exactly what they want and when they want it. This can be a daunting task when there are 64 products and their variations. This means that flexibility of production is important, which is why Malaysian Mosaics has invested heavily in the logistics fundamentals and the computerized plant, which can deal with fast-changing production scenarios. Reliability is a strength that has won brand loyalty from distributors.

Constant innovation

Malaysian Mosaics has a dedicated research and development team whose role is to constantly search for new designs and methods of production—the company realizes that it is not in the tile-manufacturing business, but in the fashion and lifestyle business, where consumer preferences change quickly. This drives the company to look out for new colors, shapes, sizes, and other variables, just as a fashion house would do. The company places design teams in different countries, recognizing the need for local adaptation to their international products, and the team decides on the most appropriate variations. Under the MML master brand, the products have exciting names, such as Starfire, Silkwinds, and Millennia.

Brand personality

The brand personality traits described by the company include:

- reliability
- good dressing
- ambitious
- well-to-do businessman
- modern outlook
- concern for continuing success

The company has established itself as a regional brand first, and now sells in 52 countries. Its ambition is to become by 2001 a global brand, defined as having steady continuous sales in over 100 countries.

Brand strengths: quality, value for money, reliable high service standards, customer focus, innovation.

Case Study 5

SITRA WOOD
Building Asian brands internationally

Sitra Wood Products recognizes the importance of building brands internationally to increase its competitiveness. Developing its brand is a coherent part of its total business strategy, and it now exports its wood-based products to more than 40 countries in five continents. It has invested heavily in state-of-the-art equipment in order to produce a wide variety of high value products, and in the last 10 years has developed a strong and wide network of contacts, agents, and distributors in the global market place.

The company is positioned as a service provider and like others, faces many challenges to branding its products. Founder and Chief Executive Officer Roland Chew claims the following are the factors responsible for the successful building of the brand internationally:

- creation of a logo that symbolizes the company's core brand values—organization, reliability, creativity, innovation, environmental consciousness. The logo, based on a triangle, is also symbolic of the three points of interdependence and the foundations of success—customers, suppliers, and staff.
- internal marketing of the brand's core values to all employees of the company. This forms a major part of the total brand-building effort, because if staff have to deliver on the brand, they are required to know what they are expected to deliver.
- development of a slogan from the company to its staff, suppliers, and customers to promote a culture of creativity among all levels of staff in an effort to become a "thinking people and learning organization."
- in line with its core brand personality characteristics, Sitra Wood has tried to introduce them into everything that it does, including product development. In this way, it has projected the message to its customers that the company is environmentally conscious and innovative by giving them a wider choice of products.
- quality is an important characteristic which Asian brands must demonstrate, and obtaining the ISO 9002 certification was felt to be a testimony to the global market, especially the European Community. Quality tests are carried out at the supplier-end and at the manufacturing plant before shipping goods to buyers.
- Sitra Wood has developed a "partner relationship" with suppliers and buyers, rather than a seller–buyer relationship. As a result, it shares know-how with its suppliers and buyers of inventory control and quality management techniques, so that all parties can work more effectively and efficiently for mutual benefit.

- the company has a continual relationship with suppliers and buyers, and always communicates with each one individually, never as a homogenous group.

- on a service level, the company differentiates itself from the competition by careful selection and training. Staff are trained to be attentive, responsive, give personal service, be flexible, organized, and adaptable. They are also trained to be innovative, think of possible improvements, and adopt a truly customer-oriented view, looking for changes rather than resisting them. All of this training is to insure that the brand promise is delivered consistently.

- technology is also used for service improvement. Requirements and preferences of customers can be captured and stored in a database, and transmitted to the manufacturing plant and relevant suppliers. Buyers can track the progress of their shipment on the company's website, and after-sales service is provided by communicating with buyers and suppliers through the Internet on issues such as quality, and delivery time.

The company has taken many more initiatives to live the values, and successfully build an international brand. It is no great surprise then that many international awards have been won by Roland Chew and Sitra Wood.

Brand strengths: innovation, living the values, customer satisfaction, differentiation in a commodity market.

8

Strategic Communications for Brand Building

THE IMPORTANCE OF A BRAND COMMUNICATIONS STRATEGY

A total communications strategy is of critical importance to brand building, as it determines the effectiveness of image creation. Communications delivers the promise of the brand that consumers will experience. The tone and style of communications reflect the brand personality, and the choice of media impacts the segment penetration.

Integrated marketing communications

Communications practices are changing rapidly, and the days when advertising agencies were given a brief and produced a media plan are now receding. As markets become more fragmented, audiences more sophisticated, and technology develop so quickly, the opportunities to communicate with consumers about a brand become almost endless. Linked to this is increasing evidence suggesting that traditional advertising messages do not work anywhere close to the effectiveness with which they used to. For instance, one study revealed that 97% of respondents misunderstood at least part of two communications they saw on TV and on average 30% of the content of each communication. With print messages, another study found that at least 21% of the meaning of communications were misunderstood. And on average, it has been estimated that traditional advertising contains approximately 30 times more information than people can assimilate. So, one has to be careful with the use of advertising in its traditional forms, and should put together an integrated communications plan that makes use of a variety of ways by which to bring the brand to people's attention.

As there are many books that concentrate on traditional advertising, promotion, and public relations, these methods will not be discussed in depth here. However, they will be mentioned along with other communications methods that brand builders are using with success.

Communicating brand values and personality

The mechanics of introducing a new brand personality and positioning, and maintenance of branding consistency become an exercise in itself one of some considerable importance. In introducing a new brand personality, security, careful preparation, and speed of execution are vital. In the introduction of a new personality, there must be set in place some form of structure to oversee the many forms of brand expression.

It has already been emphasized that every communication should be true to the values of the brand and its personality. Tremendous damage can be done to the brand and its image if any part of communications is either inconsistent or inappropriate to the character of the brand.

The company, in whatever form and wherever in the world, must "speak with one voice" in support of the brand. There are many influences that can impact, positively or negatively, on a company's brand. Some of these are shown below. Consistency across all of them is essential, and should be a main focus for brand guardianship. The main influences are as follows:

- word of mouth
- employee morale
- product performance and development
- physical premises
- permanent exhibits
- packaging
- public relations
- corporate events
- affiliation and relationship programs

- promotions
- sponsorships and events
- advertising
- direct marketing
- service standards and behavior

Word of mouth

Anyone who comes into contact with the brand will probably discuss it with someone else, either friends, relatives, customers, or even competitors. Their experience of the brand becomes its reputation and its image. If they have a good experience, they will become advocates. If they have a bad experience, they will tell at least 16 other people according to research. And these 16 will tell others. And the word spreads.

Word-of-mouth comments can be very influential on purchase decisions too. It is because of this that companies with powerful brands work very hard to insure product and service quality. Nor should employees be omitted from this list. Employees can have an even greater impact on brand image. Nothing can be worse for brand image than staff saying negative things about their company or its products and services.

Employee morale

If employee morale is poor, the problem of negative comments is likely to be chronic. But not only will the word-of-mouth problem become a major concern, the resentment of staff may manifest in the brand quality standards themselves. For a service brand, it could be seen in slovenly dressing and appearance, indifferent or impolite attitudes, misinformation and even disinformation, fall in productivity, and so on. Product quality problems could be many and varied, and companies must solve these problems in their own appropriate ways. If the costs of new equipment, new uniforms, top-class training, quality procedures, friendly working environment, and up-to-date performance management appear prohibitive, consider the cost of not making things right. Not taking action on such matters could permanently damage the brands of both the company and the product or service, and in the longer term be financially disastrous.

Product performance and development

With any brand, it goes without saying that quality must be good. That is why Ford has the slogan: Quality is job one. A brand must perform at least as well as its competition. However, there is more to it than meeting the industry standards. The brand challenge is to bring themed innovation to product development. This means thinking less from the inside out, but more from the outside in, that is thinking more like a customer, and like the competitors' customers. But, the innovation has to result in niched product differentiation, and this means developing product differentiation *in the same theme as its personality*. Personality and positioning become the "raw materials," with which, given imagination, points of difference meaningful to the customer can be constructed. For example, Virgin Atlantic Airlines offers in-flight live rock'n'roll bands on its youth-targeted holiday charters. Radical, yes, but a bold and outstanding point of niched product differentiation.

Physical premises

One of the visual items by which a brand is judged is the look of its outlets, factories, headquarter buildings, and other premises. Again, consistency matters. A bank with dozens of branches all looking different, sometimes with different colors outside and inside, clearly shows that it has not given any thought to the matter. If corporate values (printed in the annual reports) concentrate on innovation and high-tech products, then old-fashioned premises will not project this, and onlookers will perceive a certain lack of seriousness about what the company says. Consistency is what people look for in others, and corporate personality should have that same attribute to give customers confidence. A tour around a dirty factory could be translated into adverse thoughts about product quality. Personality of brands is very much to do with how they look as well as how they perform.

Permanent exhibits

Closely connected with physical premises are permanent exhibitions or theme parks, which are used either to project image or deliver product. Everyone is familiar with the Disneyland-type of permanent exhibit that is actually a product, and the extent to which the company goes to make it clean, tidy, fun, innovative, etc. But other companies are now doing similar things to attract new customers and build image. Toyota, for example, has spent ¥15 billion building a Tokyo amusement park called Mega Web, which contains a concert hall, adventure rides, a Ferris wheel, a Toyota test-drive course, and old and new model displays. The aim is not just to boost the slump in sales, but to re-position Toyota to shrug off its traditional, older person's car image, and appeal more to younger buyers. Whether this alienates the older segment remains to be seen, but high profile permanent entities like this need constant attention to insure that the brand values are protected and projected well.

Packaging

Product packaging has a high impact on perceived brand identity in a similar way. Brand values, personality, and positioning should always be reflected in every detail, including product packaging. Product packaging should be part of the themed differentiation discussed earlier. With regards to personality , dressing a product is tantamount to dressing oneself. Does one want to make the right impression? Are one's clothes in keeping with one's character? A young, fun-loving brand should look the same. Packaging is so important because it is often the first thing consumers see, and it can help the brand stand out from the crowd, which may be a long, product-packed supermarket shelf.

Public relations

Public relations, sometimes called a variety of other names, including corporate affairs or corporate communications, can also be extremely influential in projecting brand identity, particularly with corporate brands. Agencies are often on retainers to help or called upon to help especially with crisis situations. They should always be fully briefed on the content and meaning of the brand platform and desired brand image. But, what is critical is that public relations is a daily process. Every press release, every corporate speech given by top managers and every publication should reflect and stress brand values. Brand image is made by consistently and persistently projecting the identity of the brand.

Every time Anita Roddick of The Body Shop speaks, the brand values are made very clear.

Corporate events

A part of public relations, the company and its brands are very much on show at corporate events, and the same rules apply. Are the venue and its décor appropriate to the character of the brand? Does the event run with precision? Is the service up to the mark? Think of every question to insure that at the end of the event, the brand image will be perceived exactly in the way the company wants it to be.

Affiliation and relationship programs

Reward and loyalty progams (sometimes called relationship marketing or customer relationship management programs) are becoming extremely popular as more companies attempt to preserve brand loyalty. The main point to remember is that the design of the program must reflect the brand personality and values. The other connected point to watch out for is that affiliation partners with whom the company has teamed up have similar brand values. Choosing the right partners is vital. One of the problems airlines face with code sharing, other affiliation agreements and alliances is that they differentiate themselves on characteristics such as service, and it then becomes very difficult to give customers a seamless experience as they change aircraft and airlines on long journeys. Airlines claim they are forced into doing this by economics in an over-supply situation, but customers are complaining. Having internal affiliation programs with clubs and cards is safer.

Promotions

Promotions are non-face-to-face activities intended to promote sales, but they can damage a brand if the wrong perception is created. The argument against promotions is that they can make a brand appear cheap. But, there are many different types of promotion that can be used such as:

- gifts with purchases
- price reductions

- contests, quizzes

- discount coupons

- free samples

- self-liquidating premiums

- gift-pack promotions

- privilege cards

- buy-one-get-one-free offers

- redemption coupons

- charity-related promotions

The criteria for getting involved with promotions is to check out whether the proposed promotion is appropriate to the brand personality and positioning. The key word for brand management is "appropriate." Always ask the question: Is what we are doing appropriate to the brand identity? For example, Ferrari never has an annual sale with a 20% discount! On the other hand, if the brand is using a cause-related positioning strategy, the execution of a charity promotion related to that cause is entirely appropriate. In adverse times such as during a recession, there is always the temptation to get rid of last season's stock or unwanted lines, even by prestige brands. The key is trying to do it without damaging the brand. The way not to do it is to hang a very large cloth banner on the outside of your building screaming "VERSACE SALE," as one retail outlet was seen to do this year in a major Asian city. Luxury-good retailers can avoid damaging promotions like this by holding invitation-only sales, for example, that take place out of the retail premises. These retailers offer such sales only to current customers (or potential ones) so the effect is to turn the discount into rewards for customer loyalty, with no damage to the brand or any related non-discounted products.

Sponsorships and endorsements

Endorsements are basically where real personalities are used to project brand personality. They are wide ranging by nature and in terms of cost. From Michael Jordan to Pavarotti, endorsements can have differing degrees of impact on the public and the bottom line. Cindy Crawford appears prominently in advertisements for Omega watches and this is a good brand fit. Elizabeth Arden's latest "new face" to represent the brand is supermodel Amber Valetta; the company must feel that she represents the total look of the brand in terms of how customers see and associate with it. Once again, the criterion is whether the choice portrays the brand values. Another consideration is the size of the "star" compared to the size of the brand. A celebrity of immense stature might eclipse the brand, and a minor celebrity might not enhance the brand image. The fit has to be right.

Sponsorships have become very popular because they can be targeted very easily at desirable market segments, sponsorship of events being the most popular. From local events to the Football World Cup, sponsorship of sporting and lifestyle events are proving to be good for brand building. They are particularly good in the building of a brand's personality, as people watching the events identify with the sports personalities and through them associate with the brand. Decisions must be taken carefully to reinforce the brand values and positioning. Marlboro, for example, with its key brand personality characteristics of strength and independence, would probably not sponsor synchronized swimming or table tennis. But it would, and does, sponsor Formula One racing. Rolex attaches its brand to top-class tennis championships, and Pepsi-Cola was a major sponsor of the last Commonwealth Games in Malaysia. The exposure at these events is enormous and usually keeps out the competition, as categories of sponsorship have exclusivity. And the followers of the sports tend to buy the brands that go with them. Of course, sponsorship does not come cheap. Analysts have estimated Nike's sponsorship and marketing spend for 1998 at around US$170 million, but it undoubtedly brings results. The key points to remember are to choose events that match the brand's personality and to stay with the event or events chosen.

Apart from sponsorship of sports, arts and culture are also options. Cartier is creating fashion shows for jewelry with artistic backgrounds to associate the brand with works of art, such as paintings by Boticelli and other masters. Some sponsorships of this nature have connections with cause marketing and can give corporate brand image a boost. Sponsoring radio and television programs has been around for sometime but can build brand loyalty among target audiences that are demographically predictable. Companies can go one step further and actually produce programs that fit their brand and image, and sell advertising airtime to recoup costs. Again, as with other forms of sponsorship, the viewers who like the program tend to like the brand.

As a final example of how to link sponsorships to the target audience, Channel V, launched in India in 1994, has sponsored quiz shows, concerts, music awards, beach parties, and many other activities that have raised the brand's profile. Its positioning is music and entertainment, which is just what its target audience of 15–24-year-olds want.

Advertising

Advertising is the use of paid space in a publication or time on television, radio, or cinema. Its purpose is to persuade people to take a particular course of action or to reach a certain point of view. Above-the-line-advertising (ATL) includes press, television, radio, cinema, posters, and billboards. Below-the-line-advertising (BTL) involves direct mail, exhibitions, demonstrations, and point-of-sale materials. There is also on-line advertisements, which will be discussed in later with branding on the Internet. All of these activities represent the brand to the outside world and can have a major impact on image.

At present, advertising is a very uncertain industry. Apart from the impact of the recession causing declining revenues and loss of jobs, the real effectiveness of advertising is also being questioned. Television commercials are, according to many large companies, not having the impact on sales that they should, and are increasingly expensive. As a result, companies are diverting their money away to other media. Some companies have been persuaded to cut the length of television commercials from the normal 30–60 seconds to 20 seconds or even 10 seconds, but persuading customers to buy a brand is unlikely to be achieved in this manner.

The worst failing of much advertising in Asia is that agencies are given very unclear briefs regarding brand strategy. This is because many companies do not have a brand-strategy blueprint or platform as described in the first few chapters of the book. The agencies, on the other hand, seem to be more interested in revenue than strategy in many cases, and a great proportion of their staff—even in good times—do not have the strategic capability to help. The result of this double-edged sword is that advertising is often tactical and inconsistent with its messages. This situation is acute in Asia, where advertising is still a young industry that is packed with many young and inexperienced people.

This means that a company must really work hard to provide the strategic brief necessary to achieve the results it wants. The company's objectives will also influence the form of advertising. Is the aim of advertising to improve brand awareness, brand recall, boost sales quickly, improve corporate image, educate consumers, or achieve other outcomes? Whatever it is, brand strategy and values must not be compromised, and agencies must be forced to adhere to a clear brief.

Direct marketing

Direct marketing is where a company advertises brands and delivers goods directly to the consumer without any retail outlet. If used properly, it can be highly cost-effective. But to be successful it has to be targeted properly. Customers are identified as individuals, and the aim of direct marketing is to capture as much data as possible about individuals and store it on a database. Targeting communications from the database means that the right message can be sent to the right customer at the right time, motivating them to buy at the right place. Wastage is minimized. Unfortunately, direct marketing is not well understood, and most direct mail is poorly conceived and executed if the database management is poor. The customers see these communications as junk mail, and brand image suffers. The advantages then are:

- effective targeting of segments
- relationship building
- consumer involvement
- easily measurable responses
- customization of specific messages to specific people

However, all these advantages can be destroyed if the brand personality and values are wrongly projected. Personality is critical to the brand experience, and so it is with direct marketing where the customer is not seen. Customers will experience and interpret the brand personality through a voice, letter, or flyer.

With direct telephone marketing, for example, even a single scripted response can reflect the true, unique brand personality. Interactive mail should also communicate the brand personality, by projecting the values or characteristics using the appropriate choice of words and expressions. It should encourage customer involvement and associations by inviting them to the next step in the relationship, just as we would when writing to friends, hoping to get to know them better. And it is more than just personalizing the letter, the desire for a real relationship has to be communicated.

The next wave of direct marketing innovations involves on-line access, virtual kiosks and stores, and the Internet. Once again, it is vital not just for the customer to feel important, but that he or she experiences the brand personality. Customization of technology should allow the interface with consumers to express the brand values and characteristics that make it unique. With direct marketing, it is even harder to differentiate a brand from its competitors unless the personality element is visible and consistent.

Service standards and behavior

The customer brand experience is everything, and service quality must live up to the brand personality and positioning. This is very important, especially in the creation of a powerful corporate brand image; this book has devoted a major section (Creating the Brand Culture) to this in Chapter 5.

Finally, the importance of guarding the brand for a communications strategy can be summed up with the following sentence: Every image and every phrase included in a company's communications, the way the advertising looks and the style of language used, every touch added to the product, every niche addressed, every service provided must focus on the strategic brand platform, that is, its personality and positioning.

PROJECTING SEVERAL PERSONALITY CHARACTERISTICS OR BRAND VALUES

Some companies have several personality characteristics or values, and this can present a problem as to how to project them all. There are two ways of dealing with this problem.

First, if the brand is targeted at more than one segment, then it is very likely that the segment will have different needs and wants which can be expressed as emotional associations or desired personality image characteristics. This is especially relevant to corporate branding. For example, a telecommunications company will have many segments to deal with, but assuming there are just two—domestic households and businesses—the brand personality characteristics the company wishes to implement are:

- caring
- dependable
- innovative
- resourceful
- confident
- knowledgeable

In advertising and promotions, it is not an easy task to put every one of these six characteristics into, say, a 40- or 60-second corporate image television commercial. Looking a little closer at the two segments and subject to checking the company's personality characteristics against the customers, we would probably find that the kind of telecommunications "person" the company prefers would differ slightly. The priority characteristics for the customers involved in running businesses might be innovative, knowledgeable, resourceful, and dependable. The priority characteristics for families might be caring, dependable, and confident. Both segments might like all the characteristics (in fact, these characteristics would not have been chosen for a corporate brand unless they were acceptable to all audiences), but the emphasis will vary. In such a scenario, it would be quite easy to brief the agency on the slant to be placed on the brand personality for each segment. In this way, the company could have two brand communications strategies, each presenting the overall personality in a unique, attractive, and appropriate way to its relevant target audience.

Playing the brand-personality chord

An alternative problem that a company might face is presenting several brand personality characteristics to a single market segment. Companies targeting a global segment like youths typically face this. They might have as many as eight personality characteristics, as is the case with Levi's. The answer is to play these characteristics as one would a set of musical keys, where chords made up of various combinations of notes are played. In Figure 13, the Levi's brand chord is shown.

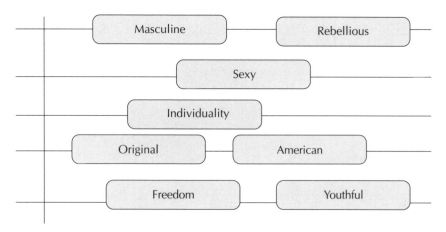

Figure 13: Levi's brand chord.

Levi's brand values are:

- masculinity
- rebelliousness
- sexiness
- individuality
- originality
- American
- freedom
- youth

What the Levi's brand does is play all the notes in various combinations over a campaign lifetime, playing up some brand personality characteristics at certain times and in certain media placements, and others on other occasions. In this way, it insures that all the brand values get a hearing with the necessary repetition over time. Repetition is needed with brand communications to keep the brand in people's minds and reinforce their perceptions. This method also gives the brand flexibility to play down some individual characteristics at times to cater for cultural sensitivities For example, the French are less sensitive about sex, but in Malaysia this value would not be appreciated so much in an advertising medium. In Germany, rebellion is tolerated more while in Japan, very much less. The brand-campaign chord can cater for these nuances, and as many as seven or eight commercials might be made for the duration of the campaign, to stress different personality characteristics of the brand. Accompanying the difference in emphasis, would also be differences in the tone and style of communications used in advertisements, to suit the brand values. (Levi's Asian brand strategy is described in full in Chapter 9).

Combining the rational and emotional messages

In presenting a brand with the various types of marketing communications, always remember to put across the rational as well as the emotional messages in order to reach both sides of the brain, and therefore stand a better chance of giving the consumer a call to action. Although it is easy for us to sort out in our minds and write down the rational and the emotional aspects of the brand, the distinction is not that clear in the consumers' minds, where the two are very much intertwined. So, the key product features and attributes must not be ignored, neither should the emotional expression. This is the skill of good creative advertising. For international branding, it should also be noted that some emotional values have more meaning and different interpretation in some cultures than in others.

Mass versus Individual communications

Mass communications in terms of addressing a global consumer segment is possible, but has more relevance for companies as opposed to products.

We know that there are global consumer segments that share similarities in many aspects, such as the high-net-worth individuals and youth. But, with products, some of the messages have to be adapted to suit different country cultures, as demonstrated with the Levi's brand chord.

Companies can more easily get a single message across with brand image advertising. Philips Electronics, for example, started a global image-building campaign in 1995 with a summary tag line: Let's make things better. Shell recently launched its first global corporate integrated communications campaign, which involves an international-issues-driven advertising campaign, a direct-mail program to opinion formers, banner advertisements on selected websites, a series of shareholder forums, and the issue of its second report on social accountability. The aim of this massive dialog with people around the world is to bring Shell's issues out into the open, and find the way forward to sustainable development, that is, balancing the needs of profit creation with care for the environment and responsibility towards affected people and communities. The end game, of course, is a good corporate image.

The point about mass communications is that it must be capable of being meaningful, acceptable, and important to every person that sees or hears it. The general trend now is towards communicating with individuals and not the masses.

Moving from mass to relationship marketing and one-to-one marketing

Relationship Marketing International sums up the trend from pluralism to individualism in marketing as follows:

Mass marketing	to	Relationship marketing
transactions		relationships
volume		value
mass production		mass customization
assumed needs		actual needs
acquisition		retention
independent contacts		integrated contacts
impersonal communications		personal communications
remote		intimate

Relationship marketing communications

The reason for the shift from pluralism to individualism is the growing ineffectiveness and cost of mass marketing allied with the low cost database technology that has led to the realization that brand value can be created through customer dialog rather than monolog. Perhaps most important of all is that in an increasingly demanding market place, improving customer retention and creating additional sales from existing customer is critical. Only extensive knowledge of customers and a deep understanding of their behavior will give a company the tools to build long-term relationships. Loyalty cards, for example, allow companies to capture individual spending and purchase behavior. This means companies can react quickly to both positive and negative changes in behavior at an individual level, and do something about it such as rewarding a high-value customer, offering extras to the most valued ones, and even re-activating lapsed customers. The result is that customer relationships are managed and controlled more effectively with a resultant increase in profit. Relationship marketing builds brand loyalty.

The trend is definitely to try and get closer to the customer in every sense, and communications presents an obvious opportunity to do this, which is why some of the better customer-relationship management programs (sometimes called relationship marketing) are enjoying a great deal of success. Effective one-to-one marketing has still a long way to go in many ways, but is certain to occupy an increasing share of the future of brand communications.

THE ONE-TO-ONE FUTURE: IMPLICATIONS FOR BRANDING

Branding and the Internet: Opportunities for Asian companies

Marketing on the Internet is, of course, one to one. According to research (and estimates vary widely), there were 130 million Internet users in mid-1998 and there are likely to be 707 million by the beginning of 2001. It is also estimated that by then trade over the Internet in the U.S. and Europe will be in excess of US$900 million, and through business-to-business marketing, more than US$100 billion of transactions would have been carried out. The increasing trend will continue well beyond 2001 and will put enormous pressures on intermediaries (wholesalers and retailers), and agencies (advertising and public relations), as more and more companies are able to deal directly with increasing numbers of consumers. This incredible technological wonder brings with it both opportunities and problems for branding— and for branding in Asia.

The main problem faced in branding will be for companies to create a special brand experience for the consumer, when there is no real face-to-face contact. At least for a while, companies are going to find it more difficult to differentiate themselves from others, personality-wise, through the computer screen, although unique websites can be created. Special attention will have to be paid to this issue, and frankly, advertising and public relations companies are not up to speed yet. They are still at the learning stage, like the rest of us, and already there are new intermediaries taking their place. Even with products, the Internet will make the tangible become intangible. So how can we get people to buy when, unlike in normal stores, they cannot feel and touch the merchandise? Some experts say that convenience and speed will count for many customers, and that the time-wasting nature of shopping will work in favor of e-commerce. In general, however, it will pose a problem of brand differentiation...a site is a site is a site, etc. It represents, therefore, an immense challenge to agency creative staff, but it is one that must be conquered as the Internet represents an interactive dialog as opposed to a non-interactive monolog with customer prospects.

With respect to Asian companies, and for that matter any small- and medium-sized businesses, Internet marketing provides great opportunities.

- For those who do not want the problems of manufacturing and distribution abroad, the Internet allows them to remove the main financial and control headaches of normal business.
- It reduces staff costs as customers do a great deal of the work themselves in brand selection and payment. It is very cheap compared to traditional methods of marketing because all customers have to do is click and buy.

- Companies can reach huge numbers of potential customers easily through the Internet, and without incurring the traditional huge marketing costs associated with building international brands. In fact, any company that can deliver on the product demand can go global in an incredibly short space of time. At the time of writing, there were over 22 million regular users of the Internet in Asia alone, and many millions more that any company can reach around the world.

- Companies involved in providing entertainment, financial services, and information, can immediately deliver their services directly to their customers.

Building a brand on the Internet

It is always advisable to seek advice from the experts, but here are a few things to think about when building a brand on the Internet. They may seem like common sense, which they are, but sometimes the basics get forgotten in the rush to keep ahead of the competition.

- The relative advantage of the Web is speed of information, and this is one of the most common benefit sought by Internet users. As more and more websites come on-line, customers will experience speed problems even though technology improves, and so will appreciate sites that give them fast loading. In fact, there are already many complaints about slow-loading sites. The implication is that a company's site should not be unattractive, but beautiful sites full of graphics turn customers off due to slow loading times

- Another point connected with ease of use is to let the customer have many navigation routes to be able to access the information they require: for example, allowing them to access information such as by product or service, applications, corporate information, latest industry news, promotions, international branches. Remember that customers are on the Web because they want to interact, so let them do it in various search forms. Search engine Yahoo! is good at this, allowing maximum interaction so that web surfers do not tune out.

- When it comes to information a company wants to put across about its brands, e.g. key messages, etc., insure that they are in an easily accessible and prominent position. Above all, a company's messages should not get lost among other people's advertisements if the company is involved with them.

- Communicate about the brand via other sites. Placing banner advertisements and securing key words with search engines so that the brand comes up first, can help build brand awareness. Make sure that there is a good brand fit—advertise only on quality sites that complement brand image.

- Do not forget the need for consistency with the brand. Logo, colors, other visuals, and the tone and style of all wording and content should reflect brand personality and values, and positioning.

- When building and upgrading the company's website, always think like a customer—make things easy for them.

USING AGENCIES

The agency brief

When using an external agency for communicating a brand or brands, it is absolutely essential that the company gives the agency a clear brief. This means giving a total view of the brand and its future, including:

- the brand's vision and mission statement (and the company's, if this is not the same)
- a statement of why consumers want the brand, or aspire to have it
- the brand personality and core values—these characteristics or values should be defined
- a brand positioning statement, which should contain a summary of why the brand is different and better than the competition

Without these items, the agency will not be able to devise creative copy that will transmit accurate key messages to the target audience. This is the main reason why so much advertising and promotion money is wasted.

If the agency gets a clear brief, it will be able to answer its own questions enabling it to get the results the company wants, such as:

- Why are we advertising?
- Who are we talking to?
- What must we say?
- How must we say it?
- Why should consumers believe it?
- What special considerations need to be accommodated?

Tag line usage

Tag lines are used by companies, often at the end of marketing communications, to summarize their position and the message they are trying to get across. Tag lines are not to be treated lightly. They may be changed, usually when there is a change in corporate strategy or direction. But if this is done frequently, it may signal to consumers that management is unsure of what it is doing or where it is heading. Tag lines should be simple to understand, yet represent differentiation that is credible, as consumers perceive them as a promise. For example, it is no use having a tag line such as "Dedicated to customer service," if customers do not experience that promise. Agencies love to come up with tag lines and can be very successful in doing so, but always check that the statement really summarizes what the brand is all about.

For example, Seiko's Kinetic watch product has the tag line: Someday all watches will be made this way. We do not necessarily believe that statement per se, but it illustrates the position it wants to own—that the watch is innovative and revolutionary. CNBC Asia's *The World is Asia's Business* neatly summarizes the business slant, the Asian emphasis, and the world context upon which all its programs are based.

Choice of agency

Choosing the right agency is not easy because at first sight, they tend to look and sound the same. One of the most important factors is to determine how strategic the agency is. Each agency will have its long client list, but not many have good strategic talent. As brand building is a strategic activity, it is essential that among the team assigned to manage the account, there is someone who has this capability. All too often, when trying to win the account, the agency's senior team turns up, but once the account has been won, unless the account is very large, the work may well be delegated to relatively junior staff. This is particularly true in Asian countries, where the industry is still fairly young.

Also of importance is the talent that turns strategy into creative communication. Good creative direction is essential, and a company should look at evidence of how well strategy has been communicated in the agency's previous work.

The size of the agency becomes an issue only if a company wants to take its brand international or global. In such a situation, the company may wish to choose an agency that is represented in those countries in order to insure consistency of communications. This is not essential if the company has a good brand guardianship process.

Communicating during a recession

Many companies severely cut their advertising and promotion budgets during times of recession or when there is a downturn in business. Prestige and luxury goods tend to be less affected, and fast-moving consumer goods tend to be affected last. Consumer durables and products such as cars tend to get hit first and to the greatest extent. However, while the need to reduce costs across the board is necessary for all companies, such times do provide an opportunity for companies to strengthen their brand image and to achieve a higher share of consumer minds. Research carried out in the U.S, Europe, and parts of Asia actually proves that increased advertising expenditure in hard times consistently provides growth in market share, sales, and profits. Levi's, for example, are still investing substantially in Asia despite the recession, because its past history shows clear and consistent gains in market share during the past recessions in Europe and the U.S.

Above all, under conditions of economic hardship, it is essential to maintain brand loyalty, and to encourage those customers of rival brands whose loyalty may be weak, to switch over to the company's brand. The cost effectiveness of brand communications can also be increased by moving away from expensive general advertising such as television commercials, to more targeted efforts aimed at these goals, for example, relationship and direct marketing activities, and below-the-line activities. Using the Levi's example again, communications expenditure is shifting to more promotional efforts, such as sponsorship of pop concerts and other value-added incentives that bring its target audience together. Promotions based on price are not to be recommended, however, as it may help sales a little in the short term, but can do permanent damage to brand image.

It is not all bad news, however, because more can be achieved for less as agencies are more willing to negotiate terms, and so the relative cost of good communications can be significantly lower. Indeed, some major companies actually use recessions to launch new products, as Kellogg's has done in Asia with its Rice Krispies Treats product.

The main message is that in times of economic adversity, a company must not stop communicating with people about its brand. In recessions, strong brands prevail.

The following case study illustrates the fact that brand image can be strengthened through non-advertising means, in SingTel's case by sponsorship and event management.

Case Study 1

SINGTEL
Enhancing brand image through
sponsorship and event management

SingTel (Singapore Telecom) often uses advertising and event sponsorship to build brand relationships. Sponsorships are felt to add another "shoulder" for the brand to stand on. However, the company is selective in what it chooses to support, and the following strategic questions are always asked before any marketing campaign is selected.

- Is the sponsorship in harmony with the brand values and personality of the company?
- Is there an opportunity to leverage on the investment through potential promotional and merchandising efforts

involving the relevant strategic business units?

- Is it aligned with the company's role as a compassionate and proactive corporate citizen?

In the last three years, SingTel has sponsored many events including:

- a National Day extravaganza, which reinforced the company image as a homegrown provider and Singapore icon
- the concert by pop group No Doubt, voted the best concert of the year (1997) and was the company's first foray into music and the youth market
- the concert by popular Hong Kong singer Sammi Cheng, which associated SingTel with perceptions of being trendy, contemporary, and in tune with the times
- a two-year sponsorship of Singapore's favorite television family sitcom, which generated many merchandising and promotional opportunities, plus incidental exposure weaved naturally into the story—neither contrived nor over-commercialized
- World Cup Soccer promotions and contests that led to thematic promotions and merchandising
- a local movie titled *Liang Po Po*, which integrated many promotional opportunities for products and image, including a shopping mall roadshow and autograph-signing sessions by the immensely popular showbiz personality

Although all of these events and some charity events have been successful (they are tracked and measured in various ways), probably the most successful of all was the Hello! Concert held in June 1998.

The Hello! Concert

The main aspects of this event are as follows:

- The Hello! concert was a breakthrough project, which integrated the resources of both the Television Corporation of Singapore and SingTel to put together an impactful and unprecedented event at the National Stadium.

- This mega concert was designed to foster goodwill with and to show appreciation to loyal customers and shareholders, and to reach out to the youths (SingTel's future customers) at the same time.

- The aim was to create a refreshing and spectacular music event that would be well-remembered by Singaporeans and tourists.

- Public response to the free tickets was overwhelming— 50,000 tickets were snapped up in less than two days.

- The concert rocked the stadium with high-energy performances by regional and international artistes such as Boyzone, KRU, and Beyond, and saw a capacity crowd of 50,000 people. The concert was also telecast "live" on national TV.

- The amount of pre- and post-media coverage dedicated to the Hello! concert was staggering and favorable. The amount of coverage had been unprecedented for what was essentially a marketing event.

- Residual effects continued to be seen in media.

- The event was voted as the best concert of the year (1998) by *Lime*, a local magazine.

This case shows that when well-planned and well-executed, sponsorship and events can be extremely rewarding, not just for product sales, but for brand image purposes also. Research carried out by SingTel has demonstrated considerable success in achieving all goals. SingTel is also a good example of how a company uses an integrated communications strategy, not relying solely on advertising and the media.

9

International Brand Acceptance in Asia

When a brand enters a market in another part of the world, no matter how well known the brand name, its success in that part of the world will depend on:

- how much effort the company puts into understanding its audience
- what it does to adjust to the distinctive needs of that audience
- how it talks to them

Perhaps the experience of brands that have successfully moved around the world can be of use to Asian brands that intend to become international. There are many issues that companies have to deal with when building a global or international brand. Throughout this book, the focus has been on the issues facing Asian companies in building powerful brands, but lessons can be learned from analyzing the Western companies that have dealt with these issues when they moved into Asia. Western companies in Asia have enjoyed enormous success in building and marketing their brands in Asia, particularly in the youth and prestige categories. It is estimated that brands like Cartier sell over half of their products to Asians.

The following case studies are examples of Western companies that have achieved success by taking new markets seriously and following the branding principles highlighted in this book. It is worth gaining an insight into what their practices are. There are two models that Western companies use to enter new markets and sustain profitable growth for

225

their brands. One is going it alone, and the other is partnering with an established Asian company. Both routes can be successful. The first case study below shows how Levi's carefully researched the Asian market and catered to the Asian youth. The TAG Heuer case shows how it is dealing with the Asian challenge. Starbucks Café is presented as another example of international brand expansion, done by choosing strategic partners in each country.

Case Study 1

THE LEVI'S STORY

Levi Strauss and Co is a company with famous global brands, but how has it managed to overcome some of the problems of gaining acceptance and leadership in another continent? As with many companies which wish to implement a multi-country strategy, a considerable amount of research is carried out to see if there are similarities or differences in what might appear to be a global consumer segment, and whether local adaptations are required. This case study examines Levi's global brand strategy and how it is integrated into the company's marketing strategy in Asia. The study also provides valuable insights into how global brands are carefully defined, managed, and communicated.

Levi's brand managers probably know as much about the global youth segment as any other in the world, as this is the segment the company primarily targets, a segment with a base of 15–19-year-old males. Indeed, the company regards one of its strategic advantages as having a better understanding of youth than any of its competitors. However, nothing is taken for granted at Levi's, and it continues to carry out consumer research every year. For example, the company conducts around 80 qualitative focus groups in Europe alone, specifically dedicated to advertising development even though such research is regarded as an aid to judgment and not a substitute for it. It is interesting to note that Levi's view of building brands in one part of the world is no different to brand building anywhere else—the same principles apply.

Research on Asian youth

Levi's has done some interesting research on Asian youth to determine similarities and differences between youth psychographics in Asia and elsewhere in the world. The results have been both interesting and valuable to Levi's Asian brand strategy. Levi's particularly looks for *similarities* in people and their perceptions of the brand. Here are some of their findings:

- The "success" formula used by Asian youth appears to be:
  - work hard at school, finish all homework, go to extra classes
  - learn to play the piano or another musical instrument
  - gain entry to university and obtain a good degree
  - work during the school holidays
  - take over the family business or be a doctor or some other professional

- There are Asian cultural restrictions that dictate that certain rules, codes, and guidelines should be observed, with respect to:
  - how to conduct oneself
  - what to consider important
  - what to strive for

In other words, belonging and responsibilities to "the group" overwhelm personal ambitions—the expectations of parents, friends, teachers, and culture surround Asian youths. These perceived expectations are so strongly felt that Asian youth fears the disappointment, disapproval, and even shame that could follow failure. This is borne out by the following two quotations:

"46% of Singaporeans believe that stress is caused by insuring that their children get good academic results."

The Straits Times, May 1998.

"Japan's rigorous academic system is also in the spotlight, as it was when there was a rash of children committing suicide in the mid-1980s and early 1990s."

"Teen violence rising in Japan," CNNI, March 1998.

The Asian recession of the late 1990s has added to the feelings of hopelessness and being out of control of one's destiny, as seen in some of the comments made by research participants:

"What's it all for?"
"Jobs are not for life any more."
"My qualifications won't count for much."

Asian youth is worried and stressed. The social issues of greatest concern to Japanese youth, for example, are crime, AIDS, and drug abuse, in that order.

However, not all is bleak; there are feelings of optimism. There is a sense of youth identity—that they are the inheritors of an exciting New World—building on an identity that is not defined or constrained by Asia's past. Young people have their own aspirations, such as:

• not having to live with their parents
• not being restricted to marrying within the race
• not having to be heterosexual
• being allowed to be themselves more

Some of the aspirational values of Asian youth, according to research, are very similar to those found around the world— though weaker or more repressed in Asia:

- an obsession with finding identity
- to overcome insecurities
- a desire to be "cool"
- a desire to be sexually attractive
- individuality

Asian youth and brands

Asian youth is particularly "brand-fickle," exhibiting

- low involvement with brand values and brand identities
- focus on newness and user values
- mass adoption, mass rejection, little repeat purchasing

They appear to be (this has not been proven by research) a bit like locusts, moving from one brand to another after avariciously devouring one. For example, with watches, they moved rapidly from Swatch to G-Shock to Baby G to AKA to Fossil to Nike. So, brand loyalty tends to suffer in the face of fashion.

But, research has found that Asian youths' views of Levi's concur with those of youth elsewhere, namely:

- authentically American
- original jeans
- quality
- cool
- self confident
- sets trends

The challenge then for companies like Levi's is how to hold back this tide of fashion change, but the similarities among world youth offers a solid foundation for consistent brand strategy.

Levi's brand values and personality

The Levi's personality is composed of eight characteristics or values with emotional associations, defined as follows:

- original—Levi's created the jeans market and is recognized as the most authentic jeans brand. Levi's, therefore, follows no one. Whenever the brand communicates to its audience, it must be seen as distinctive and original. Levi's writes its own rules and is never afraid to break them in order to remain original.

- masculine—Levi's has a masculine personality. It was designed for men engaged in hard physical labor. Male toughness and "cool" are central to the brand's character.

- sexy—Levi's has always made men and women look more attractive. It exudes a charisma and confidence that is magnetic. The attraction is not due simply to external appearance, but also to the brand's resourcefulness and intelligence.

- youthful—Levi's came of age when it was adopted by American youth in the 1950s and jeans became the uniform of the disaffected teenager. Whoever the wearer is today, jeans-wearing will always be intimately associated with youth.

- rebellious—Levi's should never be seen as part of the Establishment accepting its rules and regulations. Rules are by definition imposed by a previous generation, and the brand should always be prepared to challenge conventional behavior.

- individual—Levi's should never be afraid to stand out in a crowd and attract the attention of others. The brand has a certain confidence and integrity which means that, although it commands the respect of its peers, it has the strength of character to go it alone if necessary.

- free—Levi's travels light. It is unburdened by the clutter and hassle of everyday life and the sort of responsibilities and commitments that may hinder its freedom of action.

- American—Levi's was originally worn by the heroes who pioneered America and mapped out the American Dream. Levi's speaks with an American accent, but it does not try to force American ideology and values on others.

Levi's brand role for Asian youth

These brand values represent a particularly aspirational way of life for youth all over the world. In addition, in Asia, these values are particularly appealing given that Asian youth does not have access to the more liberal lives of Western youth. The Levi's brand is one of the few voices, which Asian youth is hearing, that is not suggesting Asian youth needs to slavishly follow the traditional Asian ways. In this respect, the brand takes some pressure off these youth and draws their empathy as a result.

Levi's brand rational associations

In addition to the brand personality, Levi's has a set of rational associations that also has to be communicated as part of a left-right brain strategy. The rational associations are:

- original—Levi's has innovated throughout the history of jeans. Levi's products will lead the way in redefining jeans and jeans-related apparel.
- simple—Levi's will always prefer a simple solution to a complicated one. Levi's seeks to eliminate the unnecessary so that the necessary can speak.
- strong—Levi's products will not be distracted from their tasks by a light knock or scrape. They are tough, strong, and resilient.
- reliable—Levi's products do not let people down. They set about their task with quiet efficiency day in and day out, week in and week out.
- long-lasting—Levi's products last for years. They are life-long companions and share their owner's experiences, achievements, and frustrations.

Levi's brand positioning

From the combination of the brand's personality and values, and its rational associations, the positioning for the brand is derived. The Levi's brand positioning (sometimes referred to as the brand soul), is embodied in the statement: The original and definitive American jeans (rational) that celebrates all the great things about being young (emotional). The ultimate anti-fashion statement.

Levi's product mission

Levi's even has a product mission: To enhance brand equity through

- maintaining the gold standard in authentic jeans and jeans-related products
- innovating and redefining within these areas
- achieving outstanding quality in everything we do.

Targeting youth in Asia

Levi's acknowledges that young people make their own decisions as to which brands to buy and that these decisions are influenced by a mixture of rational and emotional appeal. But, Levi's also agrees that peers and role models that youths look up to, with respect to both their beliefs and behavior, influence all young people. There is, therefore, a targeting hierarchy that exists, as shown in the Figure 14.

Opinion leaders certainly influence their peers in all markets, and youth is no exception. They will trigger buying by Early Adopters, and the brand (particularly fashion brands) will then be picked up by Late Adopters, and lastly, the Mass Market. There is a trickle down over time.

The Levi's brand strategy is not to appeal directly to the consumers most responsible for volume, rather to aim at opinion formers and peer group leaders, including the top portion of early adopters. This might seem rather odd when

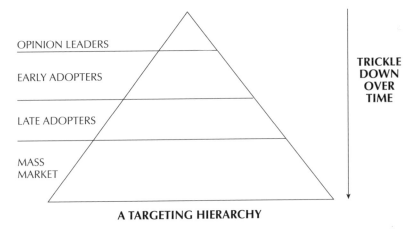

OPINION LEADERS

EARLY ADOPTERS

LATE ADOPTERS

MASS
MARKET

TRICKLE
DOWN
OVER
TIME

A TARGETING HIERARCHY

Figure 14: A targeting hierarchy.

logic would suggest the reverse, trying to influence the bulk of the market not to take new brands. Levi's say that the top end of the triangle is their "creative target" whose thoughts and actions will be overheard by the "broader target." If the creative target can be convinced to keep Levi's in their wardrobe, then the rest will do the same. And Levi's found that the opinion leaders often kept classic brands in their wardrobe as well as the latest fashion brands. Research sampling, therefore, reflects the creative target rather than the user base.

Brand communications strategy and local adaptation

Levi's created a communication mission statement to summarize the task: To enhance brand equity by finding fresh and innovative ways of communicating to consumers Levi's Core Associations, both rational and emotional.

By doing this, everyone involved in brand communications has to focus on the mission and values. There is no room for error.

Levi's always stays true to its brand personality despite incredibly different and very creative ways of portraying this. The first thing it did when entering Asia was to re-establish and reconfirm the brand values. However, like any sensitive global brand it does make adjustments for local circumstances. On a broad scale, recognizing that the advertising culture is less sophisticated in Asia and that people do not see some of the innuendoes and subtleties that would be perceived in the West, Levi's made the messages more literal. Nevertheless, Levi's produces a range of advertisements that play the Levi's brand-value chord differently depending on cultural differences. For instance, as rebellion in Japan is not culturally acceptable, that value is played down. All of the values are rotated carefully in an integrated communications strategy, so that over time the audience is exposed to all of them. (Chapter 8 gives a fuller explanation of this way of projecting brand values.) In targeting the opinion leaders, Levi's also put on events for them, on an invitation-only basis, and the words the company uses are always the language that the opinion leaders themselves use.

The results

Levi's has certainly done well in Asia among the 15–29-year-olds, as recent brand research shows.

Brand measure	Ranking
Quality	1st
Sexy	1st
Cool	1st
Youthful	1st
Sets the trends	1st

Source: Global Brand Equity Study, Millward Brown International.

Future challenges

Levi's past successes do not automatically mean that the future is safe for it. As the apparel market is continually changing, Levi's strategy will erode if it is not continually refreshed and made "market-right."

Currently, Levi's observes that the global apparel market is shifting towards new fabrics, fits, and finishes. Smaller cult brands and designer labels are cashing in on these trends. The traditional denim jeans product that Levi's sells inevitably is losing the limelight in the eyes of the consumer. These trends are most marked in the U.S. and Europe. Interestingly, the Levi's brand is holding its appeal far more strongly in the Asian region.

How should Levi's respond?

Levi's strategy has never been to follow the vagaries of fashion. Creating a positioning that transcends fashion and has classic status will always be its objective. The market is circular— clothes that were popular will become popular once again— and Levi's feel confident that denim jeans will naturally recover much of their appeal. The brand has come through more stormy times, in late 1970s in Europe, for example, to emerge stronger than before.

That said, there are significant plans in place for Levi's to insure that its popularity endures. Research is playing a key role in understanding how and why consumer tastes are changing and what that means for the brand. Market segments are being re-examined, communication being retuned, and new product possibilities considered.

In Figure 15, the consumer perceptual map indicates where Levi's intends to create a portfolio of brands and sub-brands based on the two principal consumer decision-making factors. New products and new communications campaigns are central to the whole re-positioning exercise. The marketing of the brand in the Asian region may require less fundamental change as a more solid base of consumers appears to have been built in Asia.

Lessons from Levi's

Levi's is a global brand that has won acceptance in many very different cultures, and the following points are relevant to any Asian country wanting to do the same. This case also provides important learning points for those companies wishing to enter the vast Asian market.

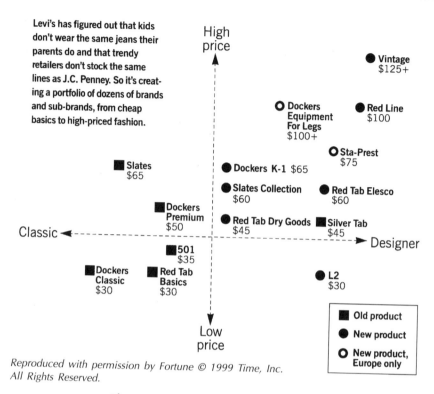

Levi's has figured out that kids don't wear the same jeans their parents do and that trendy retailers don't stock the same lines as J.C. Penney. So it's creating a portfolio of dozens of brands and sub-brands, from cheap basics to high-priced fashion.

Figure 15: Levi's: Repositioning itself.

• The same principles apply to building brands in Asia as anywhere·else in the world.
  ◆ Companies must generate consumer insight
  ◆ Having a vision or mission for the brand is vital
  ◆ Creative execution must reflect the brand personality and desired consumer associations

• Understanding the fashion dynamic in any market is critical.
  ◆ Lead, do not follow
  ◆ Target the front-end consumers
  ◆ Use research wisely, as an aid to judgment, not a substitute for it

• Appreciate the main issues affecting the brand in the market context, in this case, Asia.

(Reproduced with permission from BBH Asia-Pacific)

Levi's recent advertisement

♦ Consumers are fickle
♦ Youth is stressed

- Each company has to decide between efficiency and relevance
  ♦ Efficiency means providing one communications solution across a region, giving cost advantages, but losing some local relevance
  ♦ Relevance means providing multi-solutions for different audiences, but looking for similarities in attitudes and behaviors

Case Study 2

TAG HEUER
Breaking into Asia with a prestige brand

TAG Heuer began as Heuer in Switzerland and was founded by Edouard Heuer. The company joined the TAG Group (Techniques d'Avant-Garde) in 1985, and the joint name has become an internationally known brand that is now trying to consolidate its position in Asia. It is already established in some Asian countries, but is still trying to improve in Hong Kong and break into China. In the 1980s, it was losing money, but was turned around by the current Chief Executive Officer, Christian Viros, and his team. It now markets its products in over 100 countries.

The challenge

The turnaround challenge was to create a prestige brand, and Viros had to deal with issues as basic as:

- What are we?
- What are we not?
- Where do we want to go?

Positioning strategy

There was no clear positioning for the brand, although it did possess a degree of heritage as the Heuer company had been associated with sport for a long time, keeping official time in the 1924 Olympics Games. But in the 1980s, it stood for very little in people's minds, and was not regarded as a prestige product. It was then decided to enhance the prestige of the brand, and this meant finding a position that would clearly differentiate it from the competition. Sports was to be the catalyst for this, as no watch product at that time had linked itself to sports in a major way. Sports was also seen as the keeper of the heritage factor and as a prestigious context that could open many doors. TAG Heuer was thus positioned as The Prestige Sports Watch.

Target audience (segmentation)

TAG Heuer's sports watches and chronographs (stopwatches) are designed to appeal to both men and women who are well educated, have an international outlook, and understand the pleasure, prestige, and elegance that sports can develop and provide. They are likely to be in the age group of 18–49 years (although 20–40 years would be the main target), and either in or moving into a higher-income bracket, as prices of the products start around US$500 upwards to US$70,000^{+}. In some Asian countries, which have reached a certain level of affluence, this quality brand is not only recognized as a prestigious fashion accessory, but is also sought after by sports enthusiasts and collectors.

The brand values

The brand values of TAG Heuer on the rational side appear to be

- sturdy
- robust
- versatile

- durable
- resilient
- technical

The emotional values suggest the brand is

- precise
- challenging
- dashing
- dynamic
- risky
- tough
- heroic

Getting close to the customer

Like many brands that evolved over time without rigorous brand guardianship, TAG Heuer's distribution was in the hands of many third parties. CEO Viros decided to take back control of the brand by removing these barriers between the company and its retailers and customers. It, therefore, set up a series of subsidiary companies through which it could control the way in which the brand was marketed and get closer to the customer. Among other countries, there are subsidiaries in Hong Kong and Singapore. Country distributors account for only about 20% of product sales worldwide now.

Personality and communications

Brand personality reinforced its positioning with advertising that projected the essence of top sports persons, who were intelligent, disciplined, had mental as well as physical strength, did not crack under pressure, and were highly successful. The company has produced some outstanding advertisements, some of which have featured top sports personalities, that have consistently projected the brand personality and positioning. Athlete endorsements, sponsorship of sporting events, and fashion shows have supplemented advertising and built the brand image. The company takes a medium- to long-term view of marketing communications, especially as there has been the necessity to build brand awareness as well as establish a strong position. The company is continuing to invest in its local marketing and advertising campaigns, despite the economic recession. TAG Heuer Malaysia, for example, will continue to allocate 20% of its turnover to the advertising budget, even though revenue in 1998 was 10–12% down from that of 1997.

The Asian challenge

The longer-term view also applies to building the brand in Asia, where sports is as much a way of life as it is in Western countries. Tag Heuer is still trying to establish a strong position in Hong Kong, and is thinking through how to tackle the China market. While Asians are very brand-conscious, they are also very brand-fickle. So, while watches such as Rolex have come to represent success, the TAG Heuer brand still has to gain the perception among consumers that the attributes of sports can also demonstrate personal status and achievement. The "upscale link," as Viros calls it, is not quite there yet in some Asian countries.

Brand extensions

In the early 2000s, the company intends to move into other fashion accessories, but only ones where the products are relevant and appropriate to the brand and its values. These products would have to have substance and quality to match current brand offerings.

Brand strengths: quality, innovation, aspirational-based strategic positioning combination, leadership passion for the brand, brand advertising and promotion, brand guardianship.

Case Study 3

STARBUCKS
Changing the nature of the category

Starbucks is one of the very few companies in the world that opened up new outlets with great rapidity in a recession. In Asia, it is set to increase its number of outlets from around 150 to 500 by 2003. An international brand that started up in Seattle, Starbucks has an astonishing record of retail success in just 18 years, with basically what is a commodity product—coffee. Starbucks is very proud of what its call the Starbucks Experience. Starbucks tells us that drinking coffee is not just a normal daily activity to do; it is a drink for occasions and can be the center of a unique experience—when you want to be with your friends, need something different, or want to treat yourself. What the company has done is to completely redefine the category it is in. Everything it communicates to the market place indicates to consumers that to really enjoy coffee, they need the experience to go with it. Starbucks cuts through price barriers with the promise of the coffee-drinking experience.

Like all good retailers, location is one of Starbucks' highest priorities But Starbucks is succeeding in Asian countries like Thailand where coffee drinking has never been a favorite drink, and prices are relatively expensive. What Starbucks has done is put trendiness and fashion into a commodity product, an experience that fits the lifestyles of the 25–35 age group.

It is the brand that has the appeal, and it has been built up with consistency and reliability as two of its main pillars. As Jane Martin, International Marketing Director of Starbucks Coffee International says: "We have to protect and build the brand—everything everyone does affects it." So, the concentration of the Starbucks Experience is on coffee standards and customer service. These are the essential constants, and a customer anywhere in the world should experience the same standards of coffee and staff. This is why the essence of the brand is expressed to the staff in the words:

"One cup at a time, one customer at a time." To add value to the customer experience, Starbucks has literature on how to brew coffee and the various popular forms of drinking it, like cappuccino and latte, and about its history and the varieties of coffee beans that are grown in different parts of the world.

To Starbucks, marketing is a combination of ideas and passion. As Martin says: "We aim to provide

- the best coffee
- the best people
- respect and dignity
- a culture of passion and energy
- a commitment to the countries we are in."

To engender the passion culture, staff are called partners and receive stock options, plus a great deal of training. Everyone is taught to think like a marketer, and to understand that everyone owns the brand. The localization of the international brand comes in the form of varying the food to suit country tastes, but consistency is maintained in the green and black corporate colors, dark wood counters, signage, and other visuals.

Brand strengths: brand culture, consistency, concentration on the customer experience, location choices, local adaptation, brand guardianship.

10

Considerations for Asian Companies to Compete in the International and Global Markets

This book has been written for Asian companies that have national, international, and global aspirations. Your company may have just started on its journey, or may already be well on its way. Whatever the current position, it is always wise to look at what others are doing, particularly those that have made it to the top and achieved similar aspirations. The case studies presented in this book are a mixture of West and East, and represent different stages of brand development, and different ways of getting to their objectives. The benefits of developing global and international brands have been outlined thoroughly in the introductory chapter, so let us begin by looking at the common strategies they share.

You will also find in this chapter most of the ideas presented in the book on how Asian companies can develop powerful brands in international and global markets.

TIPS FOR BUILDING INTERNATIONAL BRANDS

Concentrate on global business categories

Global brands tend to concentrate on global business categories. They do not try to extend too far across many businesses because they are prone to failure in terms of global brand status if they do. For example, Hyundai does not hold a position in people's minds for any single

245

outstanding thing, and Virgin has brands that extended into some businesses where the name just did not have the power to carry through. Global players try not to dilute the brand, which can end up reducing the strength of the consumer relationship.

Global segments which can be exploited exist. They include the world's youth, rich people, and other groups with similar attitudes, lifestyles, opinions, and interests. Within major segments, there is always room for a small player among the giant brands that serve the segments, as long as the small player does not compete directly with them. It must not be forgotten that the multinationals have cost advantages, distribution, and other essentials that give them staying power and create barriers to entry. So, a smaller company or a new brand must have something different to offer that customers will value.

Niche marketing

Closely connected with the earlier point is finding a niche-market. Niche-markets are groups of people that have special needs that are not served by existing brands. These markets can often be found by adapting generic-type products to meet the requirements of their consumers. Research can reveal them, especially those aimed at establishing where the gaps are in the consumers' minds. Niche-markets are often profitable because consumers are prepared to pay premium prices for brands that help them as individuals to stand out from the crowd. Once established in a niche-market, it is easier for a company to defend its brand from attack. When choosing a niche-market, insure that it is sustainable in the long term and has enough volume to make it worthwhile. If possible, assess whether the idea or product has universal appeal.

Establish the strategic brand platform

Before a company promotes its brand, it should insure that the brand is firmly established with respect to its own unique personality and positioning, which will help protect it from competition and make it stand out from the crowd. Set the brand values or personality characteristics with care and define them properly so that they cannot be misinterpreted by employees and communications agencies. The company should make sure that it has a good balance of the rational and emotional aspects of its brand's identity.

Start from a strong home base, then establish a regional presence

Successful global and international brands always start from a strong home base. They are always the leading or very dominant players in their national market. And this means more than just market share. They usually have a good brand image too. Just as external customer service is never usually better than a company's internal customer service, so it is with brand image. One of the first steps then, is to make sure domestic brand image is good.

It is important to have a strong local or national brand first before foraying into the international market. Once this goal has been reached and the company is convinced it is ready to go international, the entry into foreign markets should be made in stages. Perhaps for Asian companies that do not have a vast experience of branding and international marketing, creating and managing a regional brand would be a better first step to work on. The fewer differences in values among regional countries would make brand acceptance easier. If the brand can succeed in Asia, where both population and competition are immense, then there is a better chance of gathering the experience to succeed globally. It will also help the company gain confidence and learn from the mistakes it will inevitably make with a minimum of loss. This method will also give the company time to look at more distant markets, assess potential strategic alliances, and establish the networks and contacts that will help strengthen future moves.

Innovate with discipline

World-class brands possess the capability to keep themselves fresh and new without destroying the equity and associations they have built over their lifetime. So, when a company re-invigorates its brand, it should try to stay ahead of the competition and remember never to do anything that is inconsistent or inappropriate to the brand values. Do not do anything that will not have a positive benefit to customers.

Choose and manage strategic partners carefully

In entering a foreign market, a company will need to have agreements and associations of various kinds with strategic partners, for example in distribution and manufacturing. Select them carefully so that there is not just a meeting of the minds in management terms, but also compatibility and brand fit. The partners must really understand and be committed to the brand values. Be especially careful when carrying out co-branding communications campaigns.

Adapt to local cultures and preferences where necessary

Despite employing consistent positioning, the world's best brands are sensitive to local differences, such as culture, and will adapt the brand where necessary, as long as it does not necessitate moving away from the strategic brand platform. So, they would adapt food product ingredients to take into account cultural preferences without trading off quality, as McDonald's does.

Always do some research before entering new markets, on both competitors and customers. A success in 19 countries does not mean the brand will be successful in the twentieth. Pay particular attention to cultural nuances that might mean adjustments to product and marketing.

Concentrate on the service dimension

Asian values and culture are inherently service-oriented. The very best of Asian service is the best in the world. A company should build this into its list of brand strengths, whatever business it is in. In times of recession, service excellence can be the cheapest and best way of keeping customers and promoting the brand.

Insure consistent brand positioning everywhere

Positioning is highly consistent wherever brands operate. Because positioning focuses on particular product categories, the same message is able to be projected consistently, offering the same consumer proposition to international audiences. In other words, positioning addresses similar needs, both rational and emotional. Positioning also tries to seek global market segments and looks for the similarities rather than the differences, as the Levi's case study shows.

Prepare for long-term investment

Brand building is not a short-term assignment or strategy. It takes time and huge investment. The company must, therefore, be prepared to focus both on the short and the long term. For example, it must be pre-occupied with quality, service, and short-term profit. Yet it must continue to promote its brand over the long term and guard the brand well when making short-term decisions that could affect its future, such as cutting costs that affect the customers' brand experience.

Continue to invest in the brand during adversity

Inevitably, international and global brands find that some countries suffer from recessions or economic slowdowns that affect their businesses, while other countries remain buoyant. In such circumstances, there is always pressure to reduce costs, and consequently cut advertising and promotion budgets. Leading international companies continue to invest in their brands even during harsh conditions, and have found that this pays off in terms of increases in market share and brand loyalty.

Stay true to brand values in all activities and communications— guard the brand well

Global brands always stay true to their brand values, in many cases these being the brand personality characteristics. To the power brands, this strategy is the key driver. Never do anything that is out of character with the brand. None of the world's most powerful and admired brands achieved recognition without being consistent. To consumers, consistency means trust, and trust builds brand loyalty and friendship.

Appendix: Exercises

EXERCISE 1: PERSONALITY CHARACTERISTICS

Think of two close friends, and write down all the things you like most about their personalities. Use single words to describe the values, beliefs, and characteristics that you admire in your friends. Compare how similar or dissimilar they are. Next time you see them, ask them to describe your personality in the same way. It might be interesting to share the lists.

EXERCISE IA: YIN AND YANG

List the rational and emotional aspects of your brand's attributes. Which are the most relevant and to which particular groups of customers?

EXERCISE 2: SEGMENTATION

Think of as many ways as you can as to how your product or service could possibly be used in ways different from how it is being used now. (This is a good brainstorming activity for staff meetings.). When this list is exhausted, list which market segments might be interested in any of these ideas, and what you could do to turn these matches into reality. Can you add any more value to your brand that will benefit your current customer base?

EXERCISE 2A: MARKET PLANNING AND SEGMENTATION

In which segments of market are you operating? Are they growing faster or slower than the overall market for your brand? Should you be switching emphasis for maximum growth? Have you got the right brand portfolio balance? Are the segments defined tightly defined enough? Precise definitions assist target marketing immensely.

EXERCISE 3: POSITIONING

Write down the names of three different brands that are currently appearing frequently in print or on television. Then, after looking at them, write down which positioning strategy or combination of strategies being used, and how effective it is.

EXERCISE 3A: POSITIONING

What positioning strategies are you using for your brands? Which strategies are your competitors using? Which ones are the most effective?

EXERCISE 4: BRAND EXTENSION

Using the list generated in Exercise 3, determine whether any line or brand extensions are possible through product adaptation and innovation. Can you define the target audiences for these opportunities?

EXERCISE 5: COMPETITOR ANALYSIS

Choose the two closest competitors of your company, product, or service brand, and write down a list of their brand strengths and weaknesses. Do the same for your brand. List how you can capitalize on your brand strengths, minimize or overcome its weaknesses, and improve its competitive position.

EXERCISE 6: RESEARCH

Do you know your ratings on awareness and recall in your market category? Do you know how people *feel* about your brand? Are you tracking your brand regularly against your major competitors on a regular basis? With your staff, determine which dimensions are important to customers when buying brands like yours. Draw one or more perceptual maps showing where you think your brand is in relation to the competition—put yourselves in the shoes of customers! Are there any strategic opportunities to move into good spaces? Are your competitors too close? Are you using the right positioning strategies? Think about checking this out in the market place.

EXERCISE 7: ASSESSING BRAND MARKETING EFFECTIVENESS

Consider the strength of your brand's position in your home, regional, or even international market if appropriate. Write a list of things that you have done well and not so well in marketing your brand. What can you improve upon, and how are you going to do it?

EXERCISE 8: COMMUNICATIONS

List down your brand's personality characteristics and how you would like customers to perceive your brand using any other criteria. Write another list of the ways in which you can more effectively communicate these items to your target audience.

EXERCISE 9: BRAND GUARDIANSHIP

Analyze all your brand marketing communications and events for the past year, looking for consistency and appropriateness. Have they all been true to the character of your brand, or have they differed in many ways? Where you spot inconsistencies, ask why these occurred. Is your brand guardianship process effective enough?

EXERCISE 10: NEXT STEPS

With your team or on your own, write an action plan now for your brand. What steps have you got to take over the next 12 months to strengthen your brand and make it more competitive and profitable?

Index